GCSE
Information and Communication Technology

..ouse
..d, Pride Park

P. Evans, B.Sc.(Hons)

Published by
Payne-Gallway Publishers
76-78 Christchurch Street
Ipswich IP4 2DE
Tel 01473 251097
Fax 01473 232758

E-mail info@payne-gallway.co.uk

2001

A catalogue entry for this book is available from the British Library.

ISBN 1 903112 34 6

Copyright © Phill Evans 2001

First edition 2000
Second edition 2001

Printed in Great Britain by
WM Print Ltd
Walsall
West Midlands

£11.95
04929S
14.02.02.

Acknowledgements

I would like to thank Pat Heathcote and everyone at Payne-Gallway Publishers for their help and advice in preparing this text. Special thanks go to Nick Wheat for his support and encouragement during the development of this book. I am also grateful to students and colleagues at Clough Hall Technology School for their assistance, in particular Alan Nussey for his many helpful comments and suggestions.

I am grateful to the Assessment and Qualifications Alliance (AQA)/(NEAB) Examination Board for permission to use questions from their past examination papers.

The answers in the teacher's supplement are the sole responsibility of the author and have neither been provided nor approved by the examination boards.

I would also like to thank the following organisations and individuals for permission to reproduce copyright material in the form of photographs and artwork:

M. Campbell (Figure 11.1)
T. Darlington, Vacations Travel, Stoke-on-Trent (Figure 18.1)
Evans & Sutherland Computer Corporation (Figure 21.3)
Ford Motor Company Limited (Figure 22.6)
Flora Heathcote (Figures 19.1 and 19.5)
P. Lovatt (Figure 5.3)
D. Peet & S. Faulder (Figure 3.5)
Stone Computers Ltd (Figures 1.1 and 2.6)
The Computer Desktop Encyclopaedia (Figures 2.5, 2.7, 3.3, 4.8, 5.3, 24.4)
The Met. Office (UK) (Figure 23.2, Crown Copyright material)
The Data Protection Commissioner (for extracts from the Data Protection Act reproduced in Chapter 22)
L. Tristham (Figure 14.12)

Preface

The aim of this book is to provide a clear and concise textbook covering all the necessary topics for any GCSE short or long course in Information and Communication Technology.

The book consists of 25 chapters covering all the essential material for a typical GCSE Information and Communication Technology scheme such as Specification A from The Assessment and Qualifications Alliance (AQA). Within each chapter there is sufficient material for one or two lessons along with exercises and questions from past papers. Extension work is provided at the end of each chapter through a set of relevant Web sites. A summary of the AQA Specification and advice on preparing GCSE coursework is contained in Appendices at the end of the book.

Additional exercises, answers to all the questions, MS PowerPoint presentations covering the main points of every chapter and a .html file containing the Web site URLs listed in the text are available in a separate Teacher's Supplement on the publisher's Web site http://www.payne-gallway.co.uk

Contents

Chapter 1

A computer is an **information processing machine**. Computers **process data** to produce **information**. The most common mistake made by people when they talk about computers is to believe that they are intelligent 'thinking machines'. This could not be further from the truth. Everything that a computer does depends on its being told exactly what to do and how to do it by a human.

Fig 1.1: A personal computer (picture courtesy of Stone Computers)

The sets of instructions that humans give computers are called **programs** or **software**. Without software to tell them what to do computers would be useless. Software that carries out a particular type of task for a user is often called **applications software**. Word processors, spreadsheets, databases, programs to control robots or fly aeroplanes, to calculate a company payroll or keep track of how many cans of baked beans are left in a supermarket are all examples of applications software.

There are many reasons for using computers and some of these are listed below.

- Computers can work much faster than humans can;
- Computers never get tired or need a rest;
- Computers can do jobs that it would be dangerous for a human to do;
- Computers can store large amounts of information in a very small space;
- Computers can find information very quickly;
- Computers never lose or misplace information.

Input, processing and output

Whenever a computer is used it must work its way through three basic stages before any task can be completed. These are **input**, **processing** and **output**. A computer works through these stages by 'running' a **program**. A program is a set of step-by-step instructions which tells the computer exactly what to do with input in order to produce the required output.

Input

The input stage of computing is concerned with getting the data needed by the program into the computer. **Input devices** are used to do this. The most commonly used input devices are the **mouse** and the **keyboard**.

Processing

The program contains instructions about what to do with the input. During the processing stage the computer follows these instructions using the data which has just been input. What the computer produces at the end of this stage, the output, will only be as good as the instructions given in the program. In other words, if garbage has been put into the program, garbage is what will come out of the computer. This is known as **GIGO**, or **'garbage in, garbage out'**.

Output

The output stage of computing is concerned with 'giving out' processed data as information in a form that is useful to the user. **Output devices** are used to do this. The most commonly used output devices are the **screen**, which is also called a **monitor** or **visual display unit (VDU)** and the **printer**.

Data and information

Data is any collection of numbers, characters or other symbols that has been coded into a format that can be input to a computer and processed. Data on its own has no meaning or context. It is only after processing by a computer that data takes on a context and becomes information. There are many **types** of data. Although any type of data ends up being stored as a series of numbers inside the computer, data can be input to the computer by the user in many different ways. The main types of data that can be input into a computer and processed are **numeric**, **text**, **dates**, **graphics** and **sound**.

Numeric

Numeric data types are split into two different sorts. The first is **integer**, a whole number which has no decimal point in it. The second is **real**. A real number is one with a decimal point in it. In both cases the symbols **0**, **1**, **2**, **3**, **4**, **5**, **6**, **7**, **8**, **9** are used to represent the numbers.

Text

Text data includes any character on the keyboard. Text data types are also called **string**.

Graphics

Diagrams, pictures and scanned images can be stored on a computer in special **graphics files**.

Dates

Dates are often treated as a kind of data on their own and stored inside the computer in a special way that makes them easier to process.

Sound

Any sound can be recorded in digital form for use by a computer.

A computer processes data to turn it into useful information. For example the string of numbers 13568180320003600 has no meaning. It is the correct processing of this data by the computer that transforms it into the information that "Employee number 13568 worked 36 hours in the week ending March 18th 2000". Exactly the same numbers processed in a different way could produce the information that "Student number 135 scored 68,18,3,20,0,36 and 0 in the last 7 tests".

The parts of a computer

Hardware is the name that is given to any part of a computer that you can actually touch. An individual piece of hardware is called a **device**. The basic hardware of any computer consists of a **central processing unit (CPU)** together with **input**, **output** and **backing storage** devices. The parts of a computer are shown in Figure 1.2.

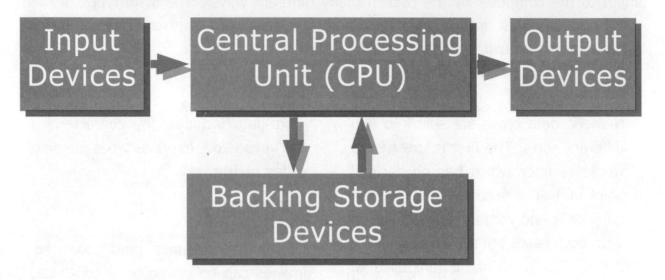

Fig 1.2: The parts of a computer.

The central processing unit (CPU)

The **Central Processing Unit (CPU)** is the part of the computer where the searching and sorting of data, calculating and decision-making goes on. The CPU is sometimes described as the 'brain' of the computer but this isn't really true because computers aren't able to think for themselves. The CPU contains the **Main Memory**, the **Control Unit** and the **Arithmetic and Logic Unit (ALU)**. The Main Memory holds the program instructions and data. It contains two types of memory chip called **ROM** and **RAM**. The Control Unit fetches instructions from the main memory, decodes them and causes them to be executed by the ALU. The ALU performs calculations and makes decisions using these instructions. Figure 1.3 opposite shows how data and instructions move around inside the CPU.

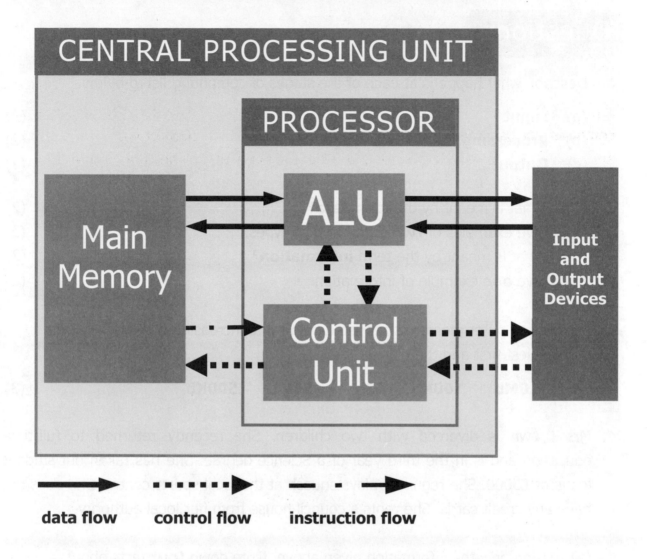

Fig 1.3: The movement of data and instructions within the CPU.

Questions

1. Describe what happens at each of the stages of computing listed below.

    (a) **Input** (2)

    (b) **Processing** (2)

    (c) **Output** (2)

2. (a) What is meant by the term **data**? (2)

    (b) Give examples of **two** different data types. (2)

    (c) What is meant by the term **information**? (2)

    (d) Give **one** example of information. (1)

3. Put the computer memory sizes listed below into increasing order of size with the smallest first and the biggest last.

    10Mb   100Kb   5Gb   50Mb   500Kb (3)

4. Mrs Brown is divorced with two children. She recently returned to full-time education and is in the third year of a Science degree. She has taken out student loans of £5000. She regularly plays squash at the local sports centre. She does not have any credit cards. She rents a council house from her local authority.

    (a) Using only the information given above, write down **four** facts about Mrs Brown which are likely to be stored in a computer database. (4)

    (b) Explain briefly the difference between information and data. (2)

    NEAB 1998 Paper 1 Tier H

Websites

- Look up definitions of the key words highlighted in this chapter using the free on-line dictionary of computing at **http://wombat.doc.ic.ac.uk/foldoc/**

- Visit **www.ai.mit.edu/people/minsky/papers/ComputersCantThink.txt** and read the article "Why people think computers can't".

- Visit the computer museum at **www.tcm.org/history** to find out about the history of computers. Try to construct a timeline to summarise the information that you find there.

Input devices are used to put data and instructions into a computer. There are two main types of input device – **direct** and **manual**.

Direct input devices can input large amounts of data quickly and accurately without any need for human intervention. **Bar code readers** and **optical mark readers** are both examples of direct input devices. These and other common direct input devices and methods are described in the next chapter.

Manual input devices are used by people to enter data by hand. The most commonly used manual input devices are the **mouse** and the **keyboard**. This chapter describes these and other commonly used manual input devices.

Keyboard

The keyboard is the most common type of input device. Ordinary computer keyboards have their keys arranged in a similar way to those on a typewriter. This way of arranging the keys is called **QWERTY** because of the order in which the keys appear on the first row of letters. Computer keyboards also have extra keys which can carry out different tasks depending upon the software that is being used.

Fig 2.1: Layout of keys on a standard QWERTY keyboard.

Some computer keyboards have a completely different set of keys and layout because of the special tasks that they have been designed for. The keys on the keyboard of a supermarket till are a good example of this — just take a look at them next time you go shopping!

Pointing devices

Fig 2.2: Some different types of mouse.

A mouse is a **pointing device**. It is the next most common type of input device after the keyboard. A mouse is moved around by the user on a flat surface next to the computer. When a mouse is moved around, a small ball underneath it turns. The mouse detects which way the ball is turning and sends data about this to the computer.

Special '**mouse driver**' software uses this data to move a small arrow around the screen. Once the user has used the mouse to point the arrow on the screen at something it can be selected by clicking a button on top of the mouse. Every mouse has at least two buttons on it. The left hand button is the one that is normally used to make selections.

Touch pads and **trackballs** are also types of pointing device. They are often used instead of a mouse on portable computers. Figure 2.3 shows a trackball attached to a keyboard being used instead of a mouse.

Fig 2.3: A trackball attached to a keyboard.

Joystick

The main use of a joystick is to play computer games by controlling the way that something moves on the screen. Joysticks can be used to control movement from side-to-side, up-and-down and diagonally. A joystick will also always have at least one button on it which can be used to make something happen like making a character in a game jump or fire a gun.

Fig 2.4: A joystick.

Touch screen

A touch screen can detect exactly where on its surface it has been touched. There are several ways in which this can be done. One common type of touch screen uses beams of invisible infra-red light which shine from top-to-bottom and side-to-side just in front of the screen. The beams of light form a grid that divides up the screen. When the screen is touched some of the beams are blocked and the exact position where the screen has been touched can be worked out by the computer. Touch screens are used in a lot of fast food chains and restaurants because they are easy to keep clean and re-program if changes need to be made to the menu.

Fig 2.5: A touch screen.

Digital camera

A digital camera can store many more pictures than an ordinary camera. Pictures taken using a digital camera are stored inside its memory and can be transferred to a computer by connecting the camera to it. A digital camera takes pictures by converting the light passing through the lens at the front into a digital image.

It does this by using a grid of tiny light sensors which convert the light that is falling on them into binary patterns of 0s and 1s. Different binary patterns are used to represent the different colours and shades of light that make up a picture. Pictures taken using a digital camera can be easily saved and transferred from one computer to another where they can be edited using special graphics software. In Figure 2.6 below, special software has been used to retrieve some pictures from a digital camera and save them onto the hard disk drive of a PC.

Some digital cameras can also capture short clips of moving images but for longer video clips a digital video camera is needed. However both of these types of camera are still quite expensive.

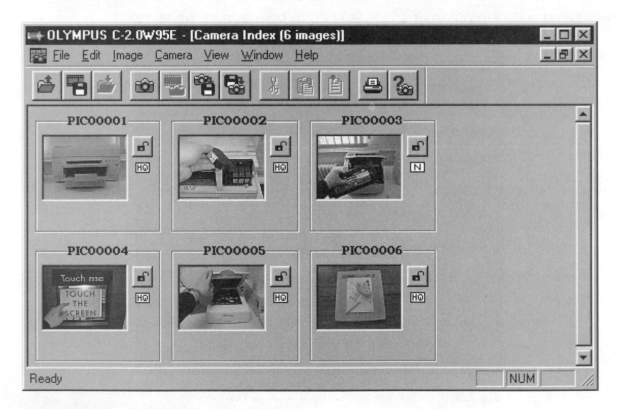

Fig 2.6: Retrieving pictures from a digital camera.

Scanner

A scanner can be used to input pictures and text into a computer. There are two main types of scanner; **Hand-held** and **Flat-bed** (shown in Figure 2.7 opposite) Scanners work by passing a beam of bright light over an image. Data is collected by sensors inside the scanner about the amount of light reflected by the different parts of the picture.

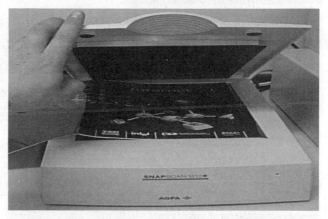

Fig 2.7: A flat-bed scanner.

This data is used to produce a digital image of the picture that the computer can display on the screen. Once the image has been scanned it can be saved and changed using special software. If text has been scanned special **optical character reading** software must be used to convert the digital image into real text. In Figure 2.8 below scanning software has been used to scan a page of printed text.

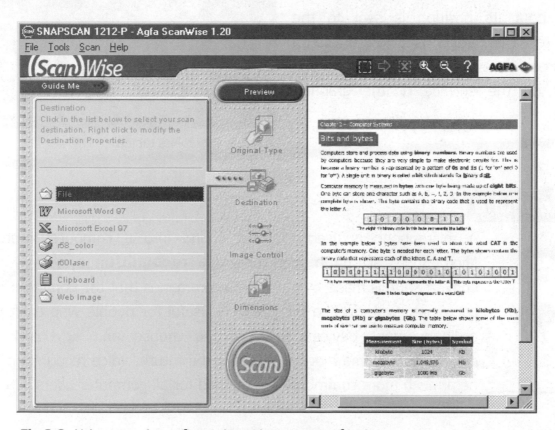

Fig 2.8: Using scanning software to capture a page of text.

Concept keyboard

A concept keyboard is a flat board with a grid of programmable keys on its surface. A single key or a group of keys can be set up to carry out a particular task. Paper overlays are placed on top of the keyboard with pictures drawn on them to represent what will happen if the keys in a certain position are pressed. Concept keyboards are often used with young children in primary schools who can't use an ordinary keyboard very well.

Graphics tablet

A graphics tablet consists of a flat surface and a pen, or stylus, which can be used to produce freehand drawings or trace around shapes. When the special pen touches the surface of the graphics tablet data about its position is sent to the computer. This data is used to produce on the screen an exact copy of what is being drawn on the surface of the graphics tablet.

Fig 2.9: A graphics tablet.

Microphone

A microphone is used to input sound into a computer system. Microphones are often used for **voice recognition** systems which convert sounds made by a user into commands that the computer can carry out. Systems like this are very useful for people who can't use ordinary input devices such as the mouse and keyboard. As computers become more powerful in the future, voice recognition will be a much more common input method for all computer users.

Light pen

A **light pen** is a small 'pen-shaped' wand, which contains light sensors. The light pen is used to choose objects or commands on the screen either by pressing it against the surface of the screen or by pressing a small switch on its side. This sends a signal to the computer, which then works out the light pen's exact location on the screen. The advantage of a light pen is that unlike a 'touch screen' it doesn't need a special screen or screen coating.

Questions

1. Tick **five** boxes to show which of the following are **input** devices.

	Tick **five** boxes only
Touch sensitive screen	
Plotter	
Motors	
CD-ROM	
Speaker	
Graphics digitiser	
VDU	
ROM	
DTP package	
Light pen	
Microphone	
Sensor	
RAM	

(5)

NEAB 1999 Paper 1 Tier F

2. (a) Explain what is meant by the term **manual input device**. (2)

   (b) Give **three** examples of manual input devices. (4)

   (c) Give **one** possible disadvantage of using a manual input device. (1)

3. For each of the tasks listed below give **one** suitable type of input device.

   (a) Entering a customer's order at the till in a fast food restaurant.

   (b) Transferring a page of printed text into a word processing program.

   (c) Teaching very young children about computers in a primary school.

   (d) Taking pictures of a school for its website.

   (e) Pointing and clicking on options on a computer screen.

   (f) Converting an old map into a digital format.

   (g) Typing a report into a word processing program. (7)

4. One of your friends is considering buying a new personal computer (PC) and has asked for your advice about the input devices that she will need.

    (a) Give **two** input devices that your friend should expect to receive as part of any standard PC package. You should explain briefly why each of these devices is needed.   (4)

    (b) Give **two** other input devices which it might also be useful for your friend to consider buying. In each case explain carefully why your friend should consider the extra expense of having these input devices as well.   (4)

Websites

- Find out more about the input devices described in this chapter by using the PC Technology Guide at **http://www.pctechguide.com/**

- Get information on the latest types of input device at **http://techshopper.com/learn/input_devices/TSH19991103S0071**

Chapter 3

Direct Input Methods

The last chapter described manual input methods, which are used by people to enter data by hand. In this chapter we will look at some methods of capturing and entering data directly without any need for human intervention. This is sometimes called **direct data entry**, or **DDE** for short and is used when very large amounts of data need to be input quickly and accurately.

Optical Mark Recognition (OMR)

Optical mark recognition, or **OMR**, uses an input device called an **optical mark reader** to detect marks made in certain places on specially printed forms. OMR is a fast input method, used where large amounts of data need to be input quickly. It is used to input data from things like answer sheets for multiple choice exams and registration forms in schools. The most common use of OMR in the UK is to input data from National Lottery forms: a National Lottery playslip is shown below. When the player has marked their choice of numbers on the playslip it is fed into the lottery terminal. OMR is used by the terminal to input the numbers from the playslip so that they can be printed on the ticket and transmitted to lottery headquarters.

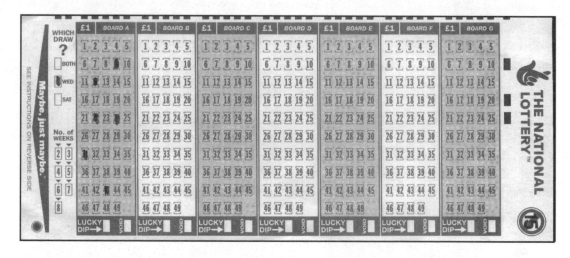

Fig 3.1: Marks on National Lottery playslips are input at lottery terminals using OMR.

Magnetic Ink Character Recognition (MICR)

Magnetic ink character recognition, or **MICR**, uses an input device called a **magnetic ink character reader** to input characters that have been printed in special magnetic ink. Banks use MICR to process cheques. The numbers along the bottom of a cheque are printed in magnetic ink. When cheques are paid into a bank the staff have to type in the amounts onto them by hand so that they can be printed on the bottom of the cheque in magnetic ink. Cheques that have been processed in this way are sent to special cheque clearing centres where they can be processed automatically in very large batches using magnetic ink character readers. Banks use this method of input for processing cheques because it is very secure. The equipment needed to print and read characters in magnetic ink is very expensive and it is unlikely that anyone would go to the trouble of trying to get hold of some just to forge cheques.

Fig 3.2: Characters are printed in magnetic ink at the bottom of a cheque. The groups of numbers represent the **cheque number**, the **sort code** (this identifies the branch that issued the cheque) and the **account number**. The amount written on the cheque is printed on it in magnetic ink once it has been paid into a bank.

Optical Character Recognition (OCR)

Optical character recognition, or **OCR**, is the use of an ordinary scanner and special software to convert text in a scanned image into a format that can be edited by word processing software. Text that is going to be input using OCR must be printed or written very clearly because poorly shaped or unclear text won't be recognised. OCR is also used for the reading of typed postcodes when mail is automatically sorted. Payment slips accompanying credit card payments are also read using OCR. The main difference between OCR and OMR is that OCR depends on the shape of the marks whereas OMR depends on the position of the marks.

Bar codes

A bar code is a set of lines of different thicknesses that represent a number. **Bar Code Readers** are used to input data from bar codes. Most products in shops have bar codes on them. Bar code readers work by shining a beam of light on the lines that make up the bar code and detecting the amount of light that is reflected back. Many bar code readers use the light from a laser beam to scan the bar code but others, such as **light pens**, use an ordinary beam of light. Bar codes don't store any information about the price of a product. They represent a code number for a product. This number can be split up into different parts that can be used to look up information about a product such as its price, size and manufacturer on a shop's computer system. It is not only shops that use bar codes; many libraries now use bar codes on their books and membership cards.

Magnetic stripe readers

A magnetic stripe is just a thin band of magnetic tape similar to the tape inside a music cassette. The most common place that you'll come across a magnetic stripe is on the back of a credit or debit card (Figure 3.3). Magnetic stripes are also used on identity cards and electronic key cards in hotels and businesses. Some schools register their students using identity cards with a magnetic stripe on them. To register, students simply swipe their card through a magnetic stripe reader. The computer identifies each student by reading the identity number from the magnetic stripe on their card. Magnetic stripes can hold only a small amount of data and are quite easy to forge. In the next few years magnetic stripes will be replaced with smart cards which store much more data on a small microchip built into the surface of the card.

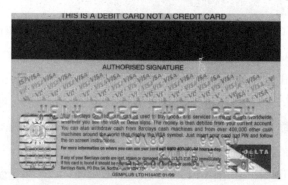

Fig 3.3: A magnetic stripe on a debit card
(the magnetic stripe is the black band at the top of the card).

Sensors

Sensors are used to detect physical quantities outside a computer such as temperature, pressure and light. To be able to process input from sensors a device called an **analogue-to-digital converter** must be connected between the computer and the sensors. This device converts signals from sensors into digital data that the computer can process.

Data logging

Data logging is a way of using a computer to automatically collect data over a period of time without any need for human supervision. Data logging is useful when data needs to be collected in remote or inhospitable conditions where it would be difficult for humans to take measurements. Weather monitoring stations are a good example of this where data often needs to be collected in places like mountain tops. Another common use of data logging is in science experiments. Some experiments need measurements to be taken either very quickly and accurately over a short period of time or slowly over a long period of time.

Whatever the application is, once the data has been collected it can be transferred anywhere using communications links like satellites and telephone lines. Once the 'logged' data has been transferred it can be analysed by computers at its final destination.

The main advantages of using data logging to gather data rather than traditional manual methods are:-

- Readings are much more accurate;
- Data can be logged over any period of time without the need for human intervention;
- Humans are released from boring, time-consuming and repetitive work.

Data is 'logged' either directly by the computer through an **input-output port**, or remotely by a **'data logger'** using **sensors** or **probes**. A data logger is a microprocessor-controlled device which can automatically collect and store data. In both of these cases the data that is being logged is usually about some **physical quantity**, such as temperature or pressure, which can have any number of different values. This produces **analogue data** which data loggers transform into **digital data** using an **analogue-to-digital converter**.

Fig 3.4: Converting analogue data from sensors into digital data.

Whatever it is that is being logged there are two important factors to be considered. These are the **period of logging** and the **time interval** between logging. The period of logging is the total time for which the data is going to be logged. The time interval is the amount of time that passes between measurements. The period of logging and the time interval chosen will depend upon the type of process which is being logged.

The stages of data logging

The process of collecting data using data logging can be broken down into a number of different stages which are described below.

- **Set up the equipment.**
  This might simply involve putting some apparatus together in a laboratory and connecting sensors to it. If data is being collected remotely the site must be visited and equipment installed including a communications link across which data can be transferred.

- **Set the period of logging and time interval.**

- **Collect data at the set time intervals throughout the logging period.**

- **Transfer the collected data to a computer.**

  In the case of remote data logging this will be through a communications link such as a telephone line or satellite connection. If data has been collected locally data is normally transferred through a direct connection to a computer.

- **Analyse the collected data.**

  The collected data can be analysed in many different ways. Two of the most common methods are the use of a spreadsheet package or an application package designed for statistical analysis. If weather data has been collected this may be used as the input to a computer model and used to produce weather forecasts.

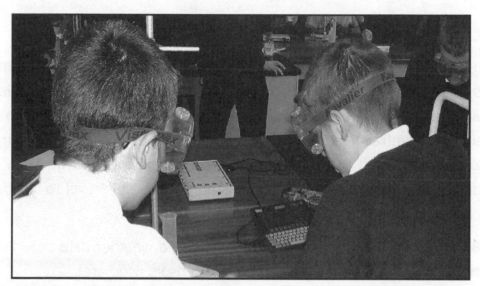

Fig 3.5: Students collecting data using portable data logging equipment.

Applications of data logging

Collecting scientific data

Taking readings during science experiments can be time consuming and tedious. Any experiment needs accurate measurements to be taken if the results are going to be of any value. Often, measurements taken by humans are not accurate because instruments are not read correctly or often enough. Data logging overcomes these problems. Experiments which use data logging need no human supervision and they can take very accurate readings, often over long periods of time, at regular time intervals. The time intervals between measurements taken by a data logger can also be much shorter than is possible for a human. Data logging in science experiments can therefore produce a much greater number of very accurate results automatically.

Monitoring hospital patients

Critically ill patients need constant monitoring and this requires the constant attention of one nurse for just one or two patients. This is often not practical or possible. Data logging can provide a solution to the problem. Patients can have their blood pressure, respiration rate, heart rate, body temperature and brain activity monitored by a data logging system. The data logger can take readings at frequent intervals and sound an alarm if any fall below a pre-set level decided upon by a doctor. As well as this constant monitoring the data logging system records the data for later analysis which can provide an accurate and up-to-date summary of a patient's condition.

Collecting weather data

Remote weather monitoring stations are used to collect data about weather conditions. Sensors are used to log and record data about physical quantities such as rainfall, air pressure and temperature. The data that is collected at each station is transferred to a central headquarters where it is combined with data from other stations to give an overall analysis of weather conditions over a large area. Collecting weather data in this way means that humans do not have to travel to locations which can often be remote and inhospitable.

Figure 3.6 opposite shows the parts of the automated weather data collection system used by the UK Meteorological Office. The main sensors used are:

- a rain-gauge to measure the amount of rainfall;
- an anemometer to measure wind speed;
- a thermometer to measure air temperature.

A data logger collects data from these sensors and uses a modem to transfer it across a telephone line to a computer in a local office or a remote office some distance away. This system allows weather data to be collected and transferred between Met. Office computers around the country. Data collected by these automated stations is combined with information from other sources such as satellites to produce weather forecasts.

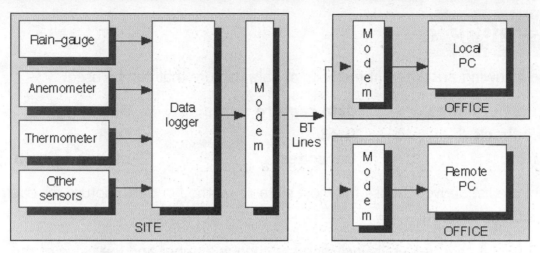

Fig 3.6: The data logging system used by the UK Meteorological Office.

Monitoring air quality

Air pollution is a growing problem especially in our cities. Data logging can help with the monitoring of air quality. Many cities now have automated air quality monitoring stations. These use data logging equipment to measure and record data about physical quantities such as pollen and carbon monoxide levels.

Questions

1. The following are different methods of data capture that can be used.

questionnaires	data capture forms	data logging
feedback	OMR	OCR
MICR	bar codes	magnetic strip

   From the list above, choose the most suitable method of data capture for each of the situations given below.

   (a) To input cheque details including the cheque number and the value of the cheque.

   (b) To input students' answers to multiple-choice examination questions.

   (c) To collect information about pupils' views on their new cafeteria system.

   (d) To capture and store temperatures every second during a chemical reaction.

   (e) To input information such as the account number from credit cards.

   (f) To input information about books being taken out of a library.   (6)

   NEAB 2000 Paper 1 Tier H

2. When cheques are paid into a bank the data on them is input to the computer system using MICR.

   (a) What is

   (i) MICR?   (1)
   (ii) OCR?   (1)

   (b) Give **two** reasons why MICR is better than OCR for this application.   (2)

   (c) If cheques are sent through the post they should not be folded.
   What problem could this cause when data is input?   (2)

   NEAB 1996 Paper 2 Tier P

3. Explain the process of data logging.   (5)

   NEAB 1996 Paper 1 Tier R

4. Describe **one** situation, other than for the collection of weather or scientific data, where data logging could be used. Your answer must include a description of the following:-

    –   **two** physical quantities that would be measured;
    –   **two** sensors that would be needed;
    –   a suitable **time interval** to leave between measurements;
    –   a suitable **period of logging;**
    –   a brief description of how the data collected would be analysed and used. (8)

5. Sensors can be attached to a computer system and used to collect data.

    In a geography investigation, students are studying how temperature varies during the course of 24 hours. A sensor is connected to a computer to take readings.

    (a) What do we call this method of data capture? (1)
    (b) (i) What kind of sensor should be used? (1)
         (ii) Why is this sensor needed? (1)
    (c) (i) How often should a reading be taken? (1)
         (ii) Why is this a suitable time interval? (1)
    (d) How could this data be presented in a report on the investigation? (1)

    NEAB 1998 Paper 1 Tier F

Websites

*   Read about how the UK Met. Office uses data logging at:
    www.meto.gov.uk/sec2/pg3/awsintro.html

*   For information about the type of data logging equipment that is used to collect weather data visit the Campbell Scientific website at:
    www.campbellsci.co.uk/products/weather/weather.htm
    This site also has some good examples of other ways that data logging has been used.

*   For information about data logging software and ideas on how to use data logging in school visit **www.dcpmicro.com/**

Chapter 4

Data is only useful as long as it is correct and up-to-date. Because of this it is important to check data when it is entered to make sure that it is both sensible and correct. If data is not checked before it is processed any errors could cause the final output to be nonsense. There are two methods that can be used to check data when it is input. These are called **verification** and **validation**.

Verification

Verification is checking to make sure that data has been entered correctly. Verification is often carried out by getting two users to enter the same set of data at different computers. Once both users have entered the data the two sets of data are compared to check that they match up. Any data that does not match up is rejected. Verification can also be carried out by software which might, for example, ask for the same data to be entered twice. If both entries don't match up the data is rejected.

Validation

Validation checks are carried out by software to make sure that data which has been entered is **allowable** and **sensible**. Data that is not sensible or allowed is rejected by the computer. There are many different types of validation check that software can make on data and some of these are described below.

Range check

Range checks are used to check that data is within a certain range of numbers or a specific set of values. For example if the examination marks for a group of students were being input, a range check could be used to make sure that each mark was greater than or equal to zero and less than or equal to the maximum possible mark.

Type check

Type checks are used to check that the correct type of data has been entered in a field. For example if numeric data is being input a type check could be used to make sure that text data isn't entered by accident.

Parity check

Sometimes when data is being transferred electronically from one place to another it can become corrupted. A parity check is used to make sure that data has not been corrupted during transmission. Data is transmitted as a binary pattern of 0s and 1s. A parity check involves adding an extra 0 or 1, called a **parity bit**, to the binary pattern so that the total number of 1s in the pattern is either an even number, which is called **even parity**, or an odd number, which is called **odd parity** — see Fig 4.1 below.

Parity Bit

In even parity the parity bit is set to either 0 or 1 so that the total number of 1s adds up to an even number. In this example there are four 1s so the value 0 is needed in the parity bit to keep the number of 1s even.

Parity Bit

In odd parity the parity bit is set to either 0 or 1 so that the total number of 1s adds up to an odd number. In this example there are two 1s so the value 1 is needed in the parity bit to make the number of 1s odd.

Fig 4.1: Even and odd parity

Hash total

Hash totals are used to check that groups of numbers have been input correctly. A hash total is the sum of a group of numbers that are going to be input. The hash total is input along with the numbers. The computer calculates a hash total for the numbers that have been input. If the hash total calculated by the computer does not match the hash total that was input with the numbers then one or more of the numbers have either not been entered or have been entered incorrectly.

Check digit

Check digits are used to validate long numbers that have a lot of digits in them. A check digit is an extra digit placed at the end of long number that can be used to check if the number has been input correctly. Check digits are often used to check numbers that have been input using direct data entry devices such as bar code scanners or light pens. The value of a check digit is worked out by performing a calculation using the individual digits that make up a number. This calculation gives the value of the check digit which is then added as an extra digit to the end of the number. Any computer can then follow the steps shown below to make sure that a number has been input correctly.

Input number including check digit at the end.

Use numbers before the check digit to re-calculate what the check digit should be.

Compare the re-calculated value of the check digit to the value that was input.

If the re-calculated check digit matches the input check digit then the number can be accepted, otherwise it must be rejected.

The best-known method of calculating check digits is the **modulus-11** system, which traps over 99% of all errors. To calculate what the check digit should be the steps listed below are followed.

1.   Each digit is assigned a weight starting at 2 with the right hand digit;
2.   Each digit is multiplied by its weight;
3.   The results of these calculations are added together to give a total;
4.   The total is divided by 11;
5.   The remainder is subtracted from 11 to give the check digit. The two exceptions are: If the remainder is 0 and the result is 11 the check digit is 0, not 11.
          If the remainder is 1 and the result is 10 the check digit is X, not 10.

E.g. To calculate the check digit for the number 1587.

original number		1	5	8	7
weights		5	4	3	2
multiply digit by its weight		5	20	24	14
add up the results		5 + 20 + 24 + 14 = 63			
divide the total by 11		5 remainder 8			
subtract remainder from 11		11 − 8 = <u>3</u> ◄— this is the check digit			

The complete code number is therefore **15873**

Length check

Length checks are used to check that input data contains a certain number of characters. For example if a value in a certain field had to contain five digits and only four digits were input, an error message would be given to the user.

Presence check

A presence check is used to make sure that a value has actually been entered in a field. In some database files entering data in certain fields can be optional. Other fields, such as key fields for example, are compulsory and must have values entered in them. A presence check makes sure that data is present in a field where it is compulsory that a value is needed.

Coding data

When data is input using a manual input device such as a keyboard, errors often occur due to values being entered incorrectly. A common mistake is to swap two letters or digits around; this is called a **transposition error**. One method that can be used to cut down on errors like this is to use **coded values** for data. Suppose that a field could contain one of three possible values; small, medium or large. Instead of typing in the full word each time we could instead type S, M or L.

Some of the advantages of coding values are:

- Fewer key presses are needed when entering a value in the field so there is less chance of the wrong keys being pressed;

- Time is saved when entering data because there is less to type in each time;

- Database packages allow automatic validation checks to be set up to make sure that only the allowed codes have been input to a field.

Coding values can also lead to problems with interpretation. Suppose three colours have the codes **B**, **G**, and **P**. Do these codes stand for 'blue, 'green' and 'pink'. Or do they represent 'black', 'grey' and 'purple' ? If these codes are interpreted incorrectly mistakes could be made when data is input.

Questions

1. Fill in the gaps in the paragraph below using the words from the following list.

correct	**presence**	**range**
digit	**processing**	**sensible**
input	**output**	**software**

   (a) Data validation is the checking of data when ...., using .... to make sure it is .... Two common methods of data validation are a .... check and a .... check. (5)

   (b) Why is the use of data validation so important? (2)

   NEAB 2000 Paper 1 Tier H

2. In a supermarket all the goods have bar codes. At the check-out the bar codes are scanned and the bar-code data is validated using a check digit.

   (a) What is a check digit? (1)

   (b) How is the check digit produced? (1)

   (c) How is the check digit used in the validation process? (3)

   NEAB 1999 Paper 2 Tier H

3. Last year a school stored all the examination marks for year 7 on a computer. Each examination had a maximum of 100 marks. At the end of the year, some pupils' examination marks were wrong when printed out. To try to stop this happening again the headteacher has decided to use data validation.

   (a) Explain what is meant by the term **data validation**. (3)

   (b) Explain how each of the following methods of data validation could be used in this situation.

   (i) Presence check (2)

   (ii) Range check (2)

   NEAB 1998 Paper 1 Tier F

4. (a) Give **two** advantages of coding data. (2)

   (b) Explain why coding data can sometimes lead to problems. (2)

5. Explain how each of the methods listed below can be used for data validation.

   (a) Parity check (3)
   (b) Type check (2)
   (c) Hash total (2)
   (d) Range check (2)

Websites

Look up definitions of the key words highlighted in this chapter using the free on-line dictionary of computing at **http://wombat.doc.ic.ac.uk/foldoc/**

Chapter 5

The programs and data needed by a computer are stored using **data storage devices**. Data storage devices can be divided into two main categories — **backing storage** and **main memory**.

Backing storage is used to store programs and data when they are not being used or when the computer is switched off. **Magnetic tape drives**, **floppy disk drives** and **hard disk drives** are all examples of **backing storage devices**. Floppy disks, hard disks, magnetic tape and CD-ROMs are all examples of **backing storage media**. These devices are used to transfer data to and from backing storage media, which is what the data is actually stored on. A backing storage device is what we use to access the data on the storage media. So a floppy disk is an example of backing storage media and a floppy disk drive is an example of a backing storage device.

When programs and data need to be used they are copied from backing storage into a collection of microchips inside the computer called the **main memory**. The two most common types of microchip, which together form the main memory of a computer, are called **ROM** and **RAM**.

Main memory

Computers store and process data using **binary numbers**. Binary numbers are used by computers because they are very simple to make electronic circuits for. This is because a binary number is represented by a pattern of **0s** and **1s** (1 for 'on' and 0 for 'off'). A single unit in binary is called a **bit** which stands for **b**inary dig**it**.

Computer memory is measured in **bytes** with one byte being made up of **eight bits**. One byte can store one character such as A, b, =, !, 2, 3. In the example below one complete byte is shown. This byte contains the binary code that is used to represent the letter A.

The eight bit binary code in this byte represents the letter **A**

In the example over the page 3 bytes have been used to store the word **CAT** in the computer's memory. One byte is needed for each letter. The bytes shown contain the binary code that represents each of the letters C, A and T.

| 1 | 0 | 0 | 0 | 0 | 1 | 1 | 1 | 1 | 0 | 0 | 0 | 0 | 0 | 1 | 0 | 1 | 0 | 1 | 0 | 1 | 0 | 0 | 1 |

This byte represents the letter **C** | This byte represents the letter **A** | This byte represents the letter **T**

These 3 bytes together represent the word **CAT**

The size of a computer's memory is normally measured in **kilobytes (Kb)**, **megabytes (Mb)** or **gigabytes (Gb)**. The table below shows some of the main units of size that we use to measure computer memory.

Measurement	Size (bytes)	Symbol
kilobyte	1,024	Kb
megabyte	1,048,576	Mb
gigabyte	1,073,741,824	Gb

ROM

ROM stands for **read-only memory**. The programs and data stored on ROM are permanent and cannot be changed. When the computer is switched off, the contents of ROM are not lost. This sort of memory which isn't wiped clean when the computer is turned off is called **non-volatile memory**.

Fig 5.1: ROM chips on an integrated circuit board.

The main use of ROM memory chips in a computer is to store the program that runs when the computer is turned on: this will then load the operating system (e.g. Windows 2000) from disk.

RAM

RAM stands for **random access memory**. RAM is the computer's 'working memory' where it stores the programs and data that are being used at a given time. The contents of RAM can be changed because it only stores programs and data temporarily. When the computer is turned off the contents of RAM are lost. This sort of memory which is wiped clean when the computer is turned off is called **volatile memory**.

PROM and EPROM

Sometimes, when new computer systems or software are being developed, special types of read-only memory that can be programmed by the software developer are required. **PROM** and **EPROM** are both special types of programmable read only memory. PROM stands for **P**rogrammable **R**ead **O**nly **M**emory.

Fig 5.2: An EPROM chip.

This type of memory can be programmed once but can't be changed again afterwards. EPROM stands for **E**rasable **P**rogrammable **R**ead **O**nly **M**emory. This type of memory can be programmed and then changed whenever necessary. It is useful for, say, developing the program which will eventually be held in ROM in a device like a washing machine or video recorder.

Hard disks

A hard disk is a circular metal disk coated with magnetic material and usually sealed in a hard disk drive inside the computer — like the one shown in Figure 5.3 below. Some hard disk drives are not permanently fixed inside the computer but are **removable**. Data stored on a hard disk can be accessed much more quickly than data stored on a floppy disk. Hard disks can store much more data than a floppy disk. A typical hard disk inside a personal computer can hold several gigabytes of data.

Fig 5.3: A hard disk drive.

Floppy disks

A floppy disk is just a circular piece of plastic coated with a magnetic material and protected by a hard plastic cover. The size of a floppy disk is measured in inches. Modern floppy disks are 3½ inches wide. A standard floppy disk can store up to 1.44 Mb of data. Floppy disks are often used to transfer small data files between computers. The parts of a floppy disk are shown in Figure 5.5 below.

The parts of a floppy disk

An outer hard plastic cover and inner woven cloth liners protect a round plastic disk coated with a magnetic material. When the disk is put into a disk drive a metal shutter slides back to reveal its surface. A small plastic write-protect tab can be clicked back to reveal a hole in the outer cover. When this tab is clicked back the disk becomes write-protected. This means that no data can be added to or removed from the disk.

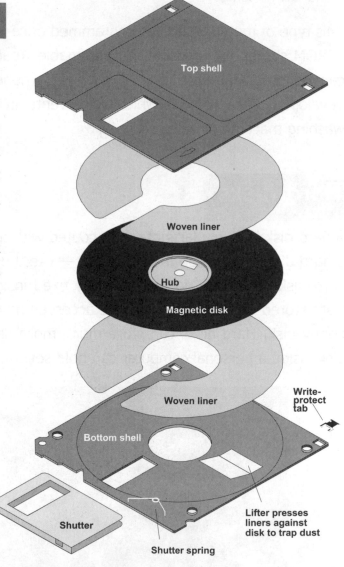

Fig 5.4: A floppy disk.

Fig 5.5: The parts of a floppy disk.

Formatting disks

Before any type of magnetic disk can be used it must be **formatted**. The process of formatting is illustrated in Figure 5.6 below, it involves:

- Deleting any data that is already on the disk. Whenever a magnetic disk is formatted any data that is already on it will be permanently erased.

- Dividing the surface of the disk into invisible circles called **tracks** which are further divided into smaller sections called **sectors**. Modern computers use high-density 3½ inch disks that are formatted with 18 sectors and 80 tracks on each side. One sector of a track can hold 512 bytes of data.

- Setting up a **root directory** where the list of files that are on the disk will be kept. Data on a magnetic disk is located by finding the **address** of its location from an **index** in the root directory. Each address in the index contains a track and sector number for an individual data segment.

- Finding any bad sectors on the disk caused by damage to the disk's surface. Data cannot be stored in these areas.

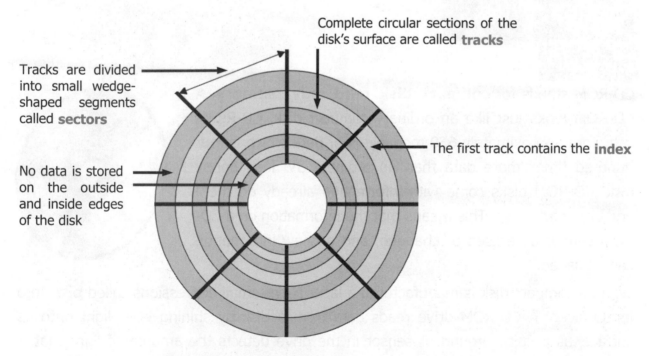

Fig 5.6: Formatting a floppy disk.

Taking care of floppy disks

Floppy disks can be damaged quite easily if they are not handled correctly. This can result in the loss or corruption of data. Some straightforward rules need to be followed to protect floppy disks.

- Never slide back the metal cover and touch the surface of the disk;

- Keep disks away from magnetic fields — for example don't put them on top of computer monitors which generate magnetic fields;

- Avoid storing disks in very hot or cold places;

- Don't keep disks in damp places or allow them to get wet;

- Don't bend disks;

- Don't lend them to other people — they could come back with files deleted or infected by viruses;

- Always label disks so that you know what's on them.

Compact disks

CD-ROM

CD-ROM stands for **compact disk read only memory**. A CD-ROM looks just like an ordinary compact disk. CD-ROMs can store approximately 650 megabytes of data which is four hundred times more data than an ordinary 3½ inch floppy disk. CD-ROM disks come with information already on them and are **read only**. This means that the information on a CD-ROM cannot be erased or changed, and no new information can be saved.

When a compact disk is manufactured a laser burns small depressions called **pits** into its surface. A CD-ROM drive reads data from a disk by shining laser light onto its surface as it spins around. A sensor in the drive detects the amount of light that is reflected back from the disk's surface. No light is reflected back from the pits. These are given the binary value 0. Light is reflected back from areas where there are no pits. These are given the binary value 1. This is how data is stored on the surface of a CD-ROM as a binary pattern of 0s and 1s.

Because of their large storage capacity CD-ROMs are excellent for storing archive material. Many newspapers produce regular CD-ROM disks that contain the complete contents of their daily editions for six months or even a year. There are also many different **multimedia** encyclopaedia titles available on CD-ROM. Multimedia means that **sound**, **pictures** and **video** are all included together on the disk as well as the ordinary text. Figure 5.7 below shows a typical multimedia encyclopaedia where videos, sound, animations and ordinary text are all available to the user.

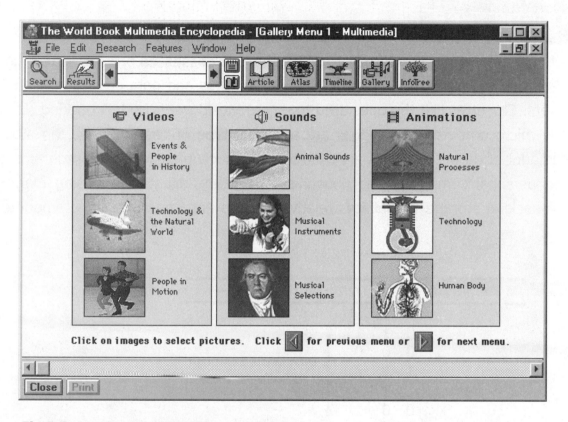

Fig 5.7: A multimedia CD-ROM encyclopaedia.

Writeable compact disks

Writeable compact disks are supplied blank and can have data put onto them using a special **read/write CD drive**. There are two main types of writeable compact disk; **WORM** (Write-Once, Read-Many) disks which can have data written to them just once, and **Magneto-Optical** disks which can have data written to them any number of times just like a hard disk.

Digital versatile disk (DVD)

DVD is the latest way of storing data. DVD discs are expected to replace ordinary compact discs and video tapes in the future. A DVD disc can store up to 17 gigabytes of data. This is enough storage space for at least four full-length feature films!

Magnetic tape

Magnetic tape comes in two forms; **tape reels**, and **cassettes** or **cartridges**. Large tape reels are used to make backup copies of programs and data on large mainframe computers. Cassettes like the ones used to record music were used as backing storage on early microcomputers. Cartridges are a special type of cassette that can store a large amount of data. Cartridges are used to make backup copies of the programs and data on personal computers and networks. The main advantage of using magnetic tape as backing storage is that it is relatively cheap and can store large amounts of data.

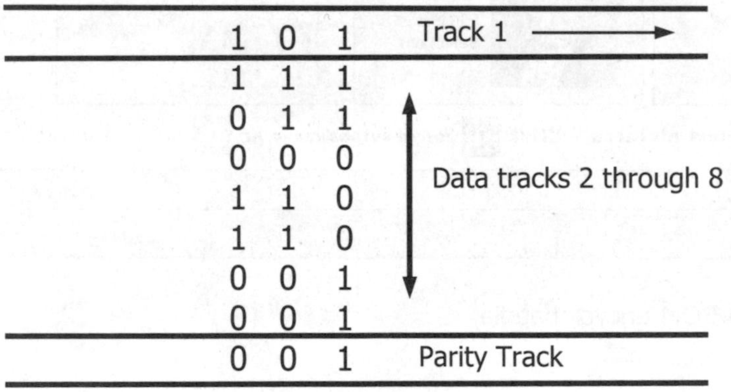

```
1   0   1     Track 1  ──────────▶
1   1   1
0   1   1
0   0   0         ▲
1   1   0         │    Data tracks 2 through 8
1   1   0         │
0   0   1         ▼
0   0   1
0   0   1     Parity Track
```

Fig 5.8: Storing data on magnetic tape.

Data is stored along the length of a magnetic tape in **tracks**, with 9 tracks being common. This gives eight **data tracks** and one **parity track**. The parity track is used to check that data has been correctly read from the tape.

Direct and serial access

Floppy disks, hard disks, CD-ROM and DVD all allow **direct access** to data. Direct access means that the required data can be found straight away without having to read through all the data on the disk. This is because the address of the correct track and sector where the data is located can be found from the index on the disk. Direct access is also called **random access** because you can read the data back in any order — not just the order in which it was first written. Magnetic tape allows only **serial access** to data. To locate data on a magnetic tape it has to be searched from the beginning until the required data is found. This is sometimes also known as **sequential access**. This makes it quite time-consuming to find and transfer data to and from magnetic tape compared with hard disks and CD-ROMs.

File compression

File compression is used to make files smaller so that more data can be stored in the same amount of space. It also makes it possible to send large files via the Internet more quickly because a compressed file is much smaller than the original file. With less data to transfer, the whole process takes less time. **File compression software** is needed to compress a file. When a compressed file on backing store needs to be used it must be **decompressed**. This can be done using **decompression software** or by setting files up to be **self-extracting** which means that they can automatically decompress themselves. **WinZip** is an example of software that can be used to compress and decompress files. Figure 5.9 shows WinZip being used to compress a collection of graphics files.

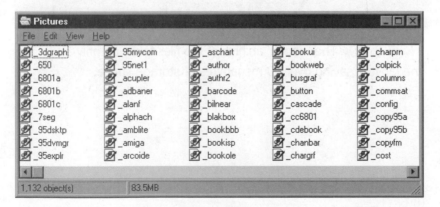

Fig 5.9 (a): This collection of over one thousand graphics files takes up 83.5 megabytes of storage space.

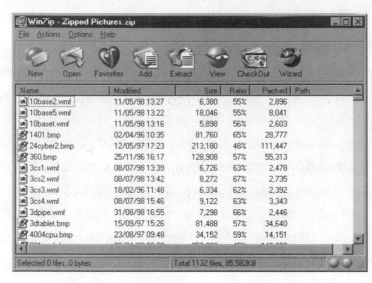

Fig 5.9 (b): WinZip software is used to compress these files.

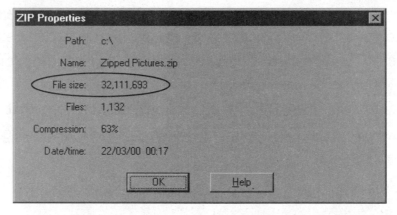

Fig 5.9 (c): The 'zipped' archive of the files takes up only 32 megabytes saving over 50 megabytes of storage space.

Questions

1. (a) How many bits are there in one **byte**? (1)

   (b) How many bytes would be needed to store one character of text data ? (1)

   (c) How many bytes would be needed to store the sentence shown below ? (Remember spaces count as characters as well!)

   The quick brown fox jumps over the lazy dog (2)

2. A member of your class has decided that their PC might be improved by using only ROM chips in its main memory because work would never be lost when the computer was switched off. Do you agree? Explain your answer. (3)

3. A computer system has two types of memory, RAM and ROM.

   (a) (i) What does RAM stand for?

   (ii) What does ROM stand for? (2)

   (b) Give **two** differences between RAM and ROM. (2)

   (c) Give **one** use of RAM. (1)

   (d) Give **one** use of ROM. (1)

   NEAB 1998 Paper 2 Tier F

4. State, with at least **one reason**, a suitable backing storage device for each task listed below.

   (a) Storing a library of clipart pictures. (1)

   (b) Making a backup copy of all the programs and data on a school network. (1)

   (c) Transferring work from the school network to your computer at home. (1)

   (d) Saving work on your computer at home. (1)

   (e) Saving a multimedia presentation that you have designed and created. (1)

5. (a) What do the letters **CD-ROM** stand for ? (1)

   (b) Explain what is meant by the term **multimedia**. (2)

   (c) Give **one** reason why CD-ROMs are used to store multimedia
   applications. (1)

   (d) Give **three** advantages that using a multimedia CD-ROM
   encyclopedia has over an ordinary printed version. (3)

   (e) What do the letters **WORM** stand for ? (1)

6. (a) Explain why computers need **backing storage**. (2)

   (b) Explain the difference between a **backing storage device**
   and a **backing storage medium**. (2)

   (c) Name **three** different types of **backing storage media.** (3)

7. An estate agent is going to transfer all of the details of her houses for sale from
   paper files to files stored on a computer.

   (a) Suggest an input device she would need to buy to input the pictures of the
   houses into the new computerised system. (1)

   The estate agent decides to store the pictures of the houses on the hard disk of
   the computer in a compressed form.

   (b) (i) Give **two advantages** of using compression in this situation. (2)

   (ii) Give **one disadvantage** of using compression in this situation. (1)

   NEAB 1998 Paper 1 Tier H

Websites

- To find out more about how a hard disk drive works
  www.howstuffworks.com/hard-disk.htm
- For the latest on Winzip software visit **www.winzip.com/**

Chapter 6

Before any output can be produced by a computer it must have an **output device** connected to it. The output devices that you are probably most used to will be the **screen**, or **monitor,** and the **printer.** Another sort of output that you will have experienced when using a computer is **sound**, which is output through a **speaker.** This chapter describes the main types of devices that are used to get output from a computer.

Monitors

A **visual display unit (VDU)** or **monitor** is an output device that accepts a video signal direct from a computer. Monitors can display graphics and text and video. The size of a monitor is measured in inches diagonally across the screen; 15, 17, 19 and 21 inch monitors are the most common sizes.

Fig 6.1: A monitor.

Monitors can be divided into three main types: **monochrome**, **grey-scale** and **colour**. A **monochrome** monitor can only display two colours, one for the background and one for the foreground. These colours are normally black and white, green and black, or amber and black. A **grey-scale** monitor is a special type of monochrome monitor that can display different shades of grey.

A **colour monitor** can display from 16 to over 1 million different colours. Colour monitors are sometimes called **RGB** monitors because they accept three separate signals — red, green and blue.

The picture on a monitor is made up of thousands of tiny coloured dots called **pixels**. The quality and detail of the picture on a monitor depends on the **resolution** it is capable of displaying. Resolution is measured in pixels going across and down the screen. A **high-resolution** monitor can show much finer detail on the screen than a **low-resolution** monitor because its pictures are made up of a much larger number of pixels. Resolutions can range from 800 x 600 to 1,600 x 1,200 pixels. Most PCs are supplied with a colour 15 inch **super video graphics adaptor** (**SVGA**) monitor with a resolution of **1,024 x 768** pixels.

Another factor which affects the quality of the image on a monitor is its **refresh rate**. This is measured in hertz (Hz) and indicates how many times per second the image on the screen is updated. To avoid flickering images which can lead to eyestrain and headaches the refresh rate of a monitor should be at least 72 Hz.

Printers

A printer is an output device that produces a printout or **hard copy** of the output from a computer. There are many different types of printer available and which one you choose will depend on how much you want to pay for the printer, the cost of the paper and ink that it uses, what quality of print you want and whether you are going to print just text, graphics, or graphics and text together. The most common types of printer are **dot matrix**, **inkjet** and **laser**.

Printers can be divided into two main categories – **impact** and **non-impact**. An impact printer produces images by striking the paper. Dot matrix printers are impact printers. A non-impact printer does not strike the paper when it is printing. Inkjet and laser printers are non-impact printers.

The quality of the image produced by a printer depends on how many **dots per inch (dpi)** it is capable of printing. A printer which can produce a large number of dots per inch will produce very clear and detailed output. The speed of printers can be measured in **characters per second** (**cps**) or **pages per minute** (**ppm**) - the higher these values are, the faster the printer can produce output.

Dot matrix printers

A dot matrix printer forms characters and graphics on the paper by producing **patterns of dots**. If you look closely at a print-out from a dot matrix printer you will see the tiny dots which make up the printout.

Fig 6.2: A dot matrix printer.

The part of the printer which forms the patterns of dots is called the **print head**. The print head is made up from **pins** which are pushed out in different arrangements to form the various patterns of dots needed. Figure 6.3 below shows a dot matrix print head.

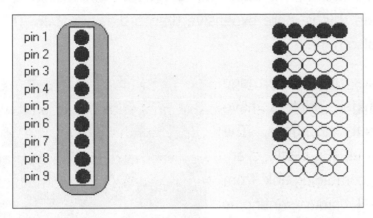

Fig 6.3: A dot matrix print head producing the letter F

Dot matrix printers are relatively cheap and so is the stationery that they use. Because they are 'impact printers' with the dots being printed by pins striking a ribbon against the paper, it is possible to print 2 or 3 copies simultaneously using 2 or 3-part stationery. The quality of dot matrix printouts depends upon how many pins there are in the print head; a **'9-pin'** printer will produce much poorer quality printouts than a **'24-pin'** printer for example. Dot matrix printers can be quite noisy and often need a special acoustic cover to reduce the amount of sound that they produce.

Inkjet printers

Inkjet printers work like dot matrix printers because the printouts that they produce are made up of patterns of very small dots but the print head has a set of tiny holes rather than pins. As the print head moves across the paper ink is forced out through the holes to form the image.

Fig 6.4: An inkjet printer.

Inkjet printers are very quiet to operate and can produce good-quality printouts of both graphics and text. Relatively cheap colour graphics can be printed using a colour inkjet. Also, inkjet printers can print on different surfaces, for example printing 'sell by' dates on food containers. However for high quality photographic images, specially coated paper is needed and this is more expensive than ordinary paper. The cost of coloured ink cartridges is also high.

Figure 6.5 opposite shows an ink cartridge being replaced. Most inkjet printers have separate black and colour cartridges. The printer shown has cartridges for black, cyan, magenta and yellow. By combining ink from the different cartridges full colour printing is made possible. To save money cartridges like these can be refilled using special commercially available refill kits.

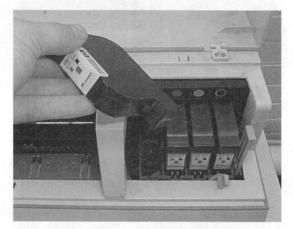

Fig 6.5: Replacing an ink cartridge.

Laser printers

Fig 6.6: A laser printer.

Laser printers give very high-quality printed output of both text and graphics very quickly and quietly. Most laser printers will produce between one and twelve pages a minute. Laser printers are generally more expensive to buy than inkjet printers and the toner cartridges are more expensive, but they are very suitable for large volume printouts because of their speed. Colour laser printers are however extremely expensive. Figure 6.7 opposite explains how a laser printer works.

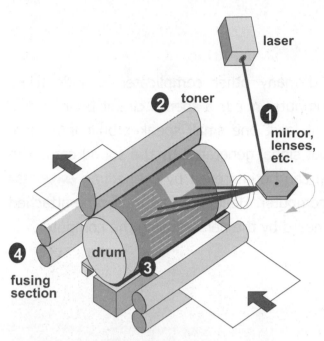

(1) The laser is used to project an image of what needs to be printed onto a cylindrical metal **drum**. It does this by heating up the drum and creating electrical charges on its surface.

(2) Special powder called **toner** sticks to the charged areas on the surface of the drum creating a 'negative image'.

(3) Paper is rolled around the drum and the toner sticks to it creating a 'positive image'.

(4) The paper is heated, permanently fusing the toner onto it.

Fig 6.7: How a laser printer works.

Reproduced from Computer Desktop Encyclopædia with permission.
(c) 1981-2000 The Computer Language Co. Inc., www.computerlanguage.com

In Figure 6.8 opposite, a drum and toner unit is being replaced. Some laser printers have separate toner cartridges which do not have the drum built in. Cartridges like these can be collected and recycled.

Fig 6.8: Replacing a toner cartridge.

Plotters

A plotter is another type of output device which will produce a hard-copy of the output from a computer. The main difference between a plotter and a printer is that a plotter uses a **pen** to draw the computer output onto the paper. Some plotters use a set of coloured pens to produce colour output. Plotters produce very accurate drawings and are often used in **computer aided design** or **CAD**.

Fig 6.9: A plotter.

Speakers

Computers can output music, voices and many other complicated sounds using speakers. To be able to output sound a computer needs a special circuit board inside it called a **sound card**. Most PCs have at least one small speaker built into them which generates sound from the audio input signal generated by the sound card. The quality and volume of the sound produced can be improved by connecting **external speakers** into a **port** at the back of the computer. Headphones can also be attached to this port so that any sound can only be heard by the person using the computer.

Questions

1. | Laser printer | Hard disk drive | MICR | OCR |
    | Dot-matrix printer | Screen (VDU) | CD-ROM | Ink-jet printer |
    | Mouse | Plotter | Scanner | OMR |
    | Keyboard | Data Validation | Speaker | Data Verification |

    Choose the **best** word from the above list to complete each of the sentences below. Write the words in the spaces provided.

    (a) A .... could be used to output a picture when a hard copy is not needed.

    (b) A firm uses a .... to produce a hardcopy of detailed accurate kitchen plans.

    (c) .... is used to mark some exams with multiple choice questions.

    (d) A .... can be used for producing invoices with carbon copies.

    (e) A .... produces a warning when a bar code is read wrongly.

    (f) .... is usually used to import moving images into multi-media computers.

    (6)

    NEAB 1998 Paper 1 Tier F

2. One of your friends is a keen artist and spends a lot of time producing drawings using their PC which is quite old. It came with a dot matrix printer and a small low resolution black and white monitor. Your friend is always complaining that this computer is no good and needs upgrading. Do you think your friend is right? Explain your answer carefully.

    (5)

3. One of your friends has decided to buy a new PC to help with her work as a graphic designer. She only has a limited amount of money to spend on a new computer and explains this to the sales assistant who suggests that buying a low-resolution monitor would save some money. Do you agree with the salesman's advice? Give at least **three** reasons to support your answer.

(4)

4. A furniture company uses a computer to help design fitted kitchens. When a customer visits the showroom a salesperson inputs their kitchen's measurements into a computer and makes suggestions about the arrangement of the various appliances and cupboards. A design is agreed and a three-dimensional illustration of how the finished kitchen will look is printed out and given to the customer.

(a) Name **one** output device that will be needed during the design stage of the kitchen planning. (1)

(b) A very accurate and high quality printout of the final design is needed for the installers to work from. Name **one** suitable **output device** that could produce this high quality plan. (1)

(c) Describe **two** advantages of producing kitchen designs in this way rather than drawing them by hand. (2)

Websites

- Find out more about the output devices described in this chapter by using the PC Technology Guide at **www.pctechguide.com/**
- Find out how dot matrix, inkjet and laser printers work by reading the article at **www.sourcemagazine.com/archive/999/feature1.asp**
- Get the latest information on output devices at these manufacturers' websites.
  Hewlett-Packard **www.pandi.hp.com/pandi-db/home_page.show**
  Epson **www.epson.co.uk/sohoprod/**
  Lexmark **www.lexmark.co.uk/**

Chapter 7

An operating system is a set of programs that controls how the hardware of a computer works. An operating system provides a means of communication between the user and the computer, deals with the loading and running of applications programs and manages the transfer of data and files to and from peripheral devices. The most widely used operating systems are called **Windows 2000**, **MacOS** (for Apple Mac computers), **Novell Netware** and **UNIX**. The operating system that a computer has also determines what applications software will run on it. Applications software will only work on a computer that has the operating system that it was designed to be used with. Applications software will not run on a computer that has a different operating system to the one that it was designed for.

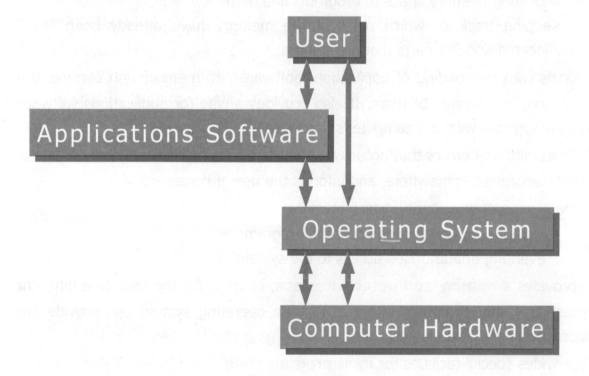

Fig 7.1: The role of the operating system.
The operating system acts as a 'bridge' between applications software and computer hardware. Users need applications software to carry out the tasks that they require. The applications software needs the operating system so that it can communicate with the hardware and get it to carry out hardware related tasks such as printing or transferring data to and from backing storage devices. Applications software and computer hardware cannot function without an operating system.

Functions of an operating system

An operating system carries out the following functions:

- It deals with input and output, which involves:

  - Accepting data from input devices and transferring it to the computer's memory.
  - Making sure that any output is sent to the correct output device.

- It manages the transfer of data between the computer's memory and backing storage devices.

- It manages system resources, which involves:

  - Allocating memory space to programs and data.
  - Keeping track of which parts of the memory have already been allocated and the parts that are still free.

- It deals with the loading of applications software into memory and controls the execution, or 'running' of them. It also provides a way for applications software to communicate with the computer's hardware.

- It deals with any errors that occur when a program is being run, or when data is being transferred somewhere, and informs the user if necessary.

- It manages system security, which involves:

  - Monitoring and restricting access to programs and data.
  - Preventing unauthorised access to the system.

- It provides a **human computer interface**, or **HCI**, for the user (the different types of human computer interface that an operating system can provide are described in the next chapter).

- It provides special facilities for **multiprogramming**.

A multiprogramming operating system can hold more than one program in memory at the same time. There are two types of multiprogramming operating system; **multitasking**, and **multiuser**.

A **multitasking** operating system allows two or more programs to run at the same time. The operating system does this by swapping each program in and out of memory in turn. When a program is swapped out of memory it is stored temporarily on disk until it is needed again. Windows 2000 is an example of a multitasking operating system. Figure 7.2 below illustrates the basic concept of a multitasking system.

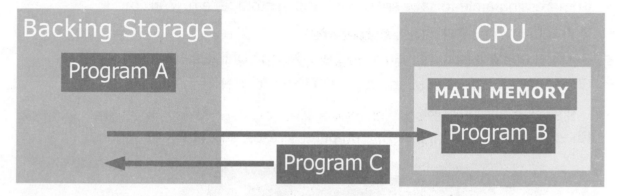

Fig 7.2: A multitasking operating system.
Program C is transferred out of main memory to backing storage as **Program B** is transferred back into main memory. **Program A** is not required yet and waits in backing storage.

A **multiuser** operating system lets many users at different terminals share processing time on a powerful central computer. The operating system does this by switching rapidly between the terminals giving each one in turn a small amount of processor time on the central computer. The operating system switches so quickly between the terminals that each user appears to have uninterrupted access to the central computer. However if there are a large number of users on such a system the time that it takes the central computer to respond can become more noticeable.

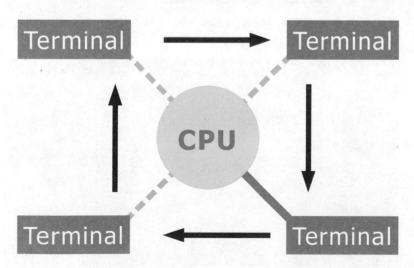

Fig 7.3: A multiuser operating system.
Each terminal in turn gets a small amount of processor time — called a '**time slice**'. Only one terminal at a time has access to the CPU.

Utility programs

Utility programs are usually supplied along with an operating system. They are used to carry out routine tasks that are often needed by a user.

Some of the routine tasks that utility programs perform are listed below.

- Compressing a file to save space on backing storage, e.g. Winzip;
- Defragmenting a disk drive, e.g. Defrag;
- Recovering data from damaged file, e.g. Norton Utilities;
- Checking a disk for faults and repairing them, e.g. Norton Utilities;
- Formatting a floppy disk;
- Checking the files on a disk for computer viruses, e.g. McAfee, Sophos;

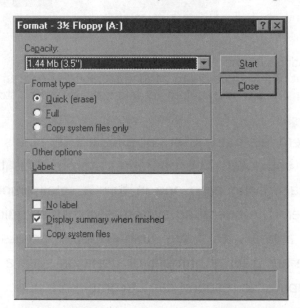

Fig 7.4: Formatting a floppy disk with a Windows utility.

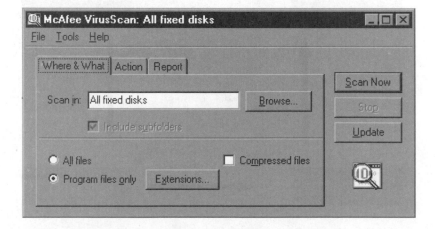

Fig 7.5: Using a virus checking utility program.

Processing methods

A **processing method** is the way that a particular operating system deals with input. There are three main types of processing method: **real-time**, **transaction** and **batch** processing. These processing methods and some examples of applications that they would be used for are described below.

Real-time processing

Real-time processing systems process input data so quickly that the resulting output can affect further input. Real-time processing is used for applications where it is essential that the computer responds straight away to input. Examples of applications where real-time processing is used are missile defence systems, automatic pilot systems on aircraft and monitoring intensive care patients in a hospital.

Fig 7.6: The flight deck of a 747 airliner — the automatic pilot must use real-time processing so that it can respond instantly to any change in the aircraft's heading, speed or altitude.

Transaction processing

Transaction, or **on-line**, **processing**, is used for applications where input needs to be dealt with straight away but it is not critical if there is a slight delay in the time that it takes for the computer to respond to requests. Examples of applications where transaction processing is used include the on-line seat booking systems used by airlines and the stock control systems used by catalogue companies like Argos. A system where transaction processing is used will always give an up-to-the-minute picture of the current situation.

Batch processing

A **batch processing** system does not respond to input straight away. Instead, input is collected together into a '**batch**' while the system is **off-line**. When a batch is ready to be processed the system goes **on-line** to carry out the processing of the data. Batch processing is non-interactive. This means that the user cannot get an immediate response to input as they would with an interactive system. Examples of applications that use batch processing include producing gas, electricity or water bills and marking OMR sheets from multiple choice examinations.

Questions

1. (a) Explain what is meant by the term **operating system**. (2)
    (b) Give **five** functions of an operating system. (5)

2. (a) What does the term **multiprogramming** mean? (1)
    (b) Explain briefly what a **multiuser** system is and how it works. (4)
    (c) Explain briefly what a **multitasking** system is and how it works. (3)

3. (a) What is a **utility program** ? (1)
    (b) Give **five** different types of task that utility programs perform. (5)

4. (a) Which **three** of the following tasks are carried out by all operating systems?

    A   transferring data to a printer
    B   allocating storage space on a disk
    C   positioning text in a word processing document
    D   finding a database record
    E   accepting keyboard input
    F   adding colour to a drawing on screen

    Write the correct letters in the spaces below

    1 _____   2 _____   3 _____ (3)

    (b) Describe an additional task which would have to be carried out by
         a **multiuser** operating system. (1)

    (c) What is a **multitasking** operating system? (2)

    NEAB 1998 Paper 2 Tier H

5. For the applications listed below give a suitable type of processing method. In
    each case support your choice of processing method with at least one reason.

    (a) Producing bills for a gas company
    (b) Controlling the automatic pilot on an aircraft
    (c) Processing cheques for a bank
    (d) Theatre seat booking system
    (g) Controlling a nuclear power station (10)

Websites

- Find out more about operating systems by visiting the sites of some of the companies that produce them.
  For UNIX **www.sco.com**
  For MacOS **www.apple.com**
  For Windows **www.microsoft.com**

Chapter 8

The human computer interface is what allows the user to communicate with the computer and is often called simply the **user interface**. The three main types of user interface are; **command-driven**, **menu-driven** and **graphical**, or **GUI**. These different types of user interface are described in this chapter.

Command-driven user interfaces

To use a command-driven system to communicate with the computer, the user has to type in special command words. DOS, which stands for Disk Operating System, is a very commonly used command-driven user interface. In the Figure 8.1 below a command-driven user interface has been used to copy a file called **fred.txt** to the user's floppy disk.

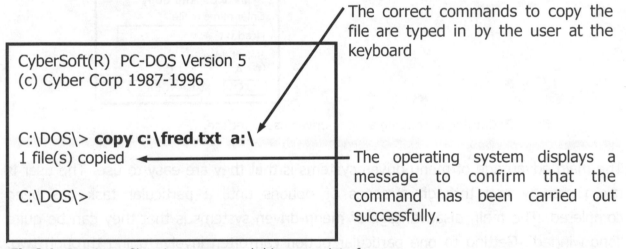

The correct commands to copy the file are typed in by the user at the keyboard

```
CyberSoft(R)  PC-DOS Version 5
(c) Cyber Corp 1987-1996


C:\DOS\> copy c:\fred.txt  a:\
1 file(s) copied

C:\DOS\>
```

The operating system displays a message to confirm that the command has been carried out successfully.

Fig 8.1: Copying a file using a command-driven user interface.

The main advantage of command-driven interfaces is that they can be quick to use as long as the user knows the correct commands. The main disadvantage of command-driven interfaces is that they are very difficult to use if the user is a beginner or doesn't know the correct commands. Command-driven systems can be very unfriendly and confusing for non-computer experts to use.

Menu-driven user interfaces

Menu-driven systems offer the user lists of options which they can select by pressing a particular key on the keyboard. Most menu-driven systems have a 'main menu' which has options on it that offer the user other menu screens once they have been selected. In Figure 8.2 below a menu-driven user interface has been used to copy a file called **fred.txt** to the user's floppy disk.

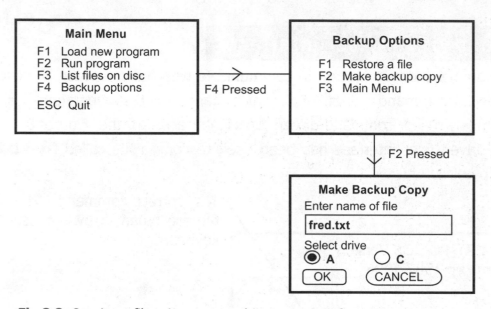

Fig 8.2: Copying a file using a menu-driven user interface.

The main advantage of menu-driven systems is that they are easy to use. The user is taken step-by-step through a series of options until a particular task has been completed. The main disadvantage of menu-driven systems is that they can be quite 'long-winded'. Getting to one particular option can often involve going through two, three or even more different menu screens.

Graphical user interfaces

The most widely used type of **graphical user interfaces** are **WIMP** systems. WIMP stands for **W**indows **I**cons **M**enu **P**ointer. Options are represented by small pictures or '**icons**' arranged inside rectangular boxes called **windows**. To choose an option represented by an icon the user uses a mouse to move a pointer on the screen over the icon and then 'double clicks' on it with the mouse button. To choose an item from a menu the user clicks on a word in the **menu bar**. This reveals a **drop-down menu** with a list of options. To choose an option the user points to it and clicks once on the mouse button. Figure 8.3 below shows **Windows**, the most widely used graphical user interface in the world today.

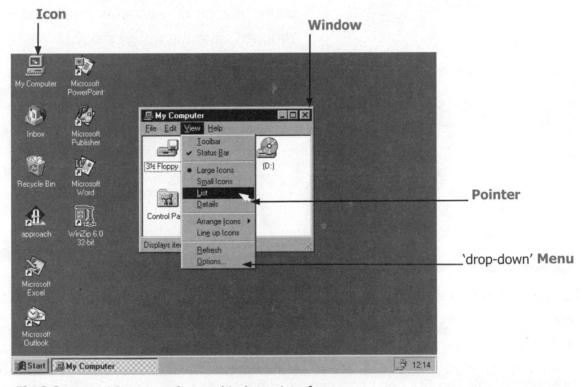

Fig 8.3: Typical features of a graphical user interface.

The main advantage of graphical user interfaces is that they are very easy to use, especially for a beginner. The main disadvantage is the amount of memory space they need. A graphical user interface like Windows needs a lot of RAM to run properly. As well as using up a lot of RAM, graphical user interfaces also take up a large amount of hard disk space.

In the Figure 8.4 below, a graphical user interface is being used to copy a file called **fred.txt** to the user's floppy disk. Copying a file is simply a case of 'dragging and dropping' the file from its current location into another window or folder.

The user points to the file that needs copying, clicks and holds down on the left-hand mouse button, and drags it across to the window which shows the current contents of the floppy disk. When the user lets go of the mouse button a copy of the file is made and 'dropped' onto the floppy disk.

In this example the file has been copied to floppy disk but a copy could have been made by pointing to it, clicking on the right-hand mouse button, and simply choosing 'copy'.

Fig 8.4: Copying a file using a graphical user interface.

User interface design

A good user interface should be **user-friendly**. This means that even inexperienced users should be able to learn how to use it quite quickly and easily. To make a user interface user-friendly care must be taken when it is being designed. Some of the factors that should be considered when designing a new user interface are:

- The way that the different parts of the user interface are operated should be consistent. This is so that when a user has learnt how to do one thing it will be easier for them to learn how to do other things in a similar way;

- The layout of the screen and the positioning of items such as windows, icons and menus on the screen should be consistent;

- Colours should be chosen that are easy to see. For example black text on a dark blue background is a poor combination. Also, colours should be chosen to be consistent with what people are used to — you would not use a green box for warning and a red box to mean 'OK — continue';

- Sound can be used to do things such as alerting the user to problems but it should also be possible to turn it off;

- On-line help is often a useful feature. This means that the user can call up help on the screen and not have to stop what they're doing to refer to a manual.

Questions

1. (a) What is a **human computer interface (HCI)** ?   (2)
    (b) Describe **three** different types of human computer interface
         and describe at least **one** feature of each.   (6)
    (c) Give **four** factors that should be taken into account when
         designing a new human computer interface.   (4)

2. The way in which a user interacts with computer software is important. A
    good Human Computer Interface makes software easy to use.

    Explain how the user makes choices in each of the following types of interface.

    (a) A graphical user interface.   (2)
    (b) A menu-driven user interface.   (2)
    (c) A command-driven user interface.   (1)

    NEAB 1999 Paper 2 Tier F

3. The design of the user interface of an application is very important. The two
    screens shown on the opposite page are from a package which allows
    customers to choose and book a holiday.

    (a) Describe **three** ways in which the user interface has been kept
         consistent in the two screen designs.   (3)
    (b) (i) In what ways does the design limit the choices a user can make?   (2)
         (ii) Why has the package been designed in this way?   (2)
    (c) Describe **two** changes you would make to the design which would
         make the interface easier for customers to use. Explain why these
         changes would help the user.   (4)
    (d) Sometimes holidays are fully booked for the dates required. A
         message is displayed on the screen to tell the user the holiday is not
         available.
         (i)   Where on the screen should this message appear?   (1)
         (ii)   Why is this position most suitable?   (1)
         (iii) How could the user's attention be drawn to this message?   (2)

    NEAB 1998 Paper 2 Tier H

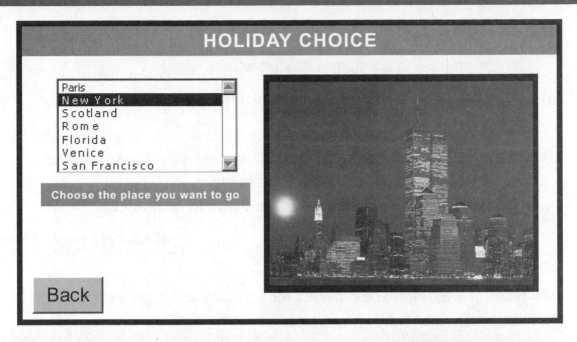

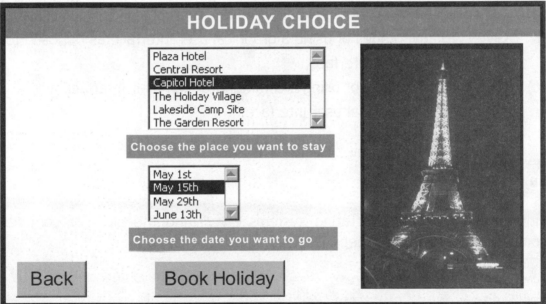

4.   Three types of user interface are:

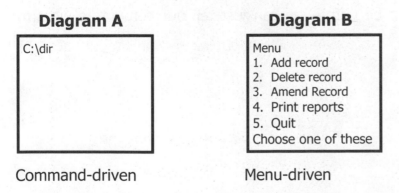

Diagram A

C:\dir

Command-driven

Diagram B

Menu
1. Add record
2. Delete record
3. Amend Record
4. Print reports
5. Quit
Choose one of these

Menu-driven

Diagram C

Graphical

(a) Give **one** reason why an inexperienced user might find the command driven interface in Diagram A difficult to use. (1)

(b) Give **two** reasons why a user might find the graphical user interface in Diagram C easier to use. (2)

(c) The menu-driven interface shown in Diagram B is still used for many applications. Describe **one** advantage to the user of this interface compared with the graphical interface shown in Diagram C. (1)

NEAB 1995 Paper 2 Tier Q

5. Two types of user interface provided for software are a graphical user interface (GUI) and a command-driven interface.

(a) List **four** items you would expect to find in a graphical user interface. (4)

(b) Give **two** advantages of using a graphical user interface as opposed to a command-driven interface. (2)

(c) Give **one** advantage of using a command-driven user interface as opposed to a graphical user interface. (1)

Websites

- Find out more about operating systems by visiting the sites of some of the companies that produce them.
  For UNIX **www.sco.com**
  For MacOS **www.apple.com**
  For Windows **www.microsoft.com**

- Links to other useful sites on user interfaces can be found at **www.acm.org/sigchi/nci-sites/**

- Visit **www.speech.be.philips.com/intro.htm** to find out about speech recognition. How long will it be before we can just tell our computers what to do?

Chapter 9 — Application Software

There are two main types of computer software; **system software** and **application software**. System software includes the operating system and utility programs and has already been discussed. Application software caries out user-related tasks and can be classified as **general-purpose**, **specialist** or **tailor-made**.

General-purpose application packages

A **general-purpose application package** is a type of software that can perform many different related tasks. Word processors, spreadsheets, databases, graphics and presentation software are all examples of application packages. This type of software is sometimes called **generic** software. This means, for example, that any one of the many different word processing packages that you could buy will all do the same general sorts of tasks as each other.

Most computer users buy application packages 'off-the-shelf'. There are several good reasons for using this type of ready-made software — some of these are listed below.

- It is relatively cheap;
- It is readily available and can be installed quickly and easily;
- It will have been thoroughly tested so there will be very little chance of it having any serious faults or 'bugs';
- It will be well supported with a lot of books available about how to use it as well as on-line help and discussions on the Internet.

The most common types of general purpose software and the types of tasks that they can be used for are listed below.

- **Database packages** (e.g. MS Access, Lotus Approach, Paradox) are used to store and retrieve information;

- **Spreadsheet packages** (e.g. MS Excel, Lotus 123) are used for tasks that involve a lot of calculations or for the production of graphs and charts;

- **Word processing packages** (e.g. MS Word, WordPerfect) are used to produce text-based documents such as letters, reports and memos;

- **Desktop publishing (DTP) packages** (e.g. MS Publisher, PageMaker, PagePlus) are used to produce professional quality publications such as posters, books, newsletters, newspapers and magazines;

- **Graphics packages** (e.g. Paint, PaintBrush, Serif Draw, Corel Draw) are used to produce and manipulate artwork;

- **Computer-aided design (CAD)** packages (e.g. 2D-Design, AutoCAD, TurboCAD) are used to produce engineering designs and architectural plans;

- **Communications software** (e.g. Internet Explorer, Netscape Communicator) is used to access the Internet and send and receive e-mail;

- **Presentation graphics packages** (e.g. PowerPoint, Lotus Freelance) are used to create slide shows and presentations which can be viewed on-screen or with a data or overhead projector;

- **Web page editors** (e.g. MS FrontPage, Macromedia Dreamweaver) are used to create Web pages.

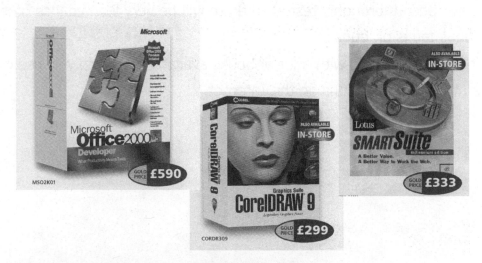

Fig 9.1: General purpose application software.

Integrated packages

An integrated package combines many different types of application together in one single package. This type of software normally offers facilities for word processing, spreadsheets, databases, graphics, presentation and communications.

The advantage of integrated packages is their cost — they are much cheaper than buying many different application packages. The main problem with them is that the different applications have a limited number of features compared with individual application packages. Microsoft WORKS is an example of an integrated package.

Integrated packages are not very common and have gradually been replaced by applications bundled together by software manufacturers and sold as suites of programs. Microsoft's Office 2000 (Figure 9.2) is an example of a bundled suite of application programs. These bundles offer the advantages of applications with a complete set of features, a common user interface and easy facilities for sharing and exchanging data.

Fig 9.2: The MS Office 2000 suite of programs — database, spreadsheet, word processing and desktop publishing software are all included. Products like this are now much more commonly used than integrated packages.

Specialist application software

Specialist application software performs a single very specific type of task. Programs to work out payroll, calculate accounts, plan driving routes (see Figure 9.3), work out income tax returns, deal with stock control and handle appointments are all examples of specialist application software.

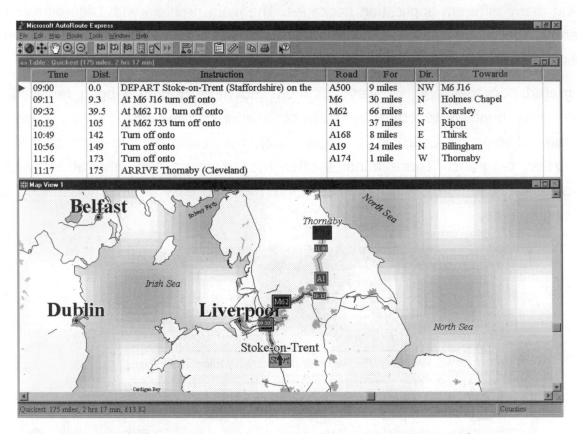

Fig 9.3: Route planning software — an example of specialist application software

Tailor-made software

Sometimes an organisation finds that 'off-the-shelf' software will not do exactly what it wants. In this case they might decide to have special tailor-made, or **bespoke** software specially developed for the purpose. The main drawbacks of this approach are the high cost and long time that some programs take to develop.

Buying new software

Before buying new software there are a number of questions, or "evaluation criteria" that need to be considered before making a final choice. Application software can be very expensive — especially for a large business that may need many copies or special licences to be able to use the software on all of their computers. Choosing the wrong software can be a very costly mistake.

Some of the questions that should be considered are:-

- What sort of tasks will the software be used for?

- How much does the software cost and how much money is available to buy it?

- What operating system does the software need? Software will only work with the operating system that it was designed for;

- What are the minimum system requirements for the software? Every application package has a minimum set of hardware requirements such as how much hard disk space and memory are needed;

- Will the software be used on a single computer or on a network? If the software is going to be used on a network a special version of it may be needed;

- How much support is available for users? This could be in the form of on-line help, telephone support lines, internet sites and printed manuals. More popular software will have more of these resources;

- How easy is the software to install — can an ordinary user carry out the installation or will an ICT expert be needed to do it?

Questions

1. Choose the most suitable type of application software to use for each of the tasks described below.

database	**spreadsheet**
word-processing	**desk top publishing (DTP)**
graphics	**communications**
data logging	**computer aided design (CAD)**

   (a) drawing a picture

   (b) storing a school's student records

   (c) producing the plans for a new building

   (d) calculating your weekly budget

   (e) writing a field-study report

   (f) organising the layout of a school newsletter

   (g) collecting data during a science experiment

   (h) sending an e-mail (8)

   NEAB 2000 Paper 2 Tier F

2. Computers need both **system software** and **applications software**.

   (a) Explain why computers need both types of software. (2)

   (b) Give **three** different categories of application software. (3)

   (c) Explain what is meant by the term **application package**. (2)

   (d) Describe briefly **five** evaluation criteria that could be used by a user when choosing a new application package for their PC. (5)

3. (a) Explain what is meant by the term **integrated package**. (2)

   (b) Give **one** advantage and **one** disadvantage of using an integrated package. (2)

   (c) Explain why integrated packages are becoming less commonly used and describe the types of products that have replaced them. (2)

4. Jean Davies owns two high street shops that sell fashion clothes and accessories aimed at teenagers. Her company already has a computer system that is used for word processing but she wants to buy software that will help her with stock control. She must decide whether to buy an existing software package or have one specially written for her company.

    (a) Give **two** advantages to her of buying an existing software package.   (2)

    (b) Give **two** advantages to her of having a piece of software specially written.   (2)

    NEAB 2000 Paper 1 Tier F

5. Explain why commercial applications packages are not always exactly suited to the needs of a business user and describe how these limitations can be overcome.   (5)

Websites

- Visit **www.egghead.com** and **www.computerworld.com** to find articles with reviews and descriptions of popular applications software. Use this information to write about the system requirements and strengths and weaknesses of the general purpose application packages that you use at school — this will be useful for your coursework.

- Visit **www.shareware.com** and **www.shareware.org** and investigate what the terms "shareware" and "freeware" mean. What are the advantages and disadvantages of using these types of software?

Chapter 10

Since the middle of the 20th Century we have used computers to store information. Before we had computers information was stored on pieces of paper or card in **manual filing systems**. A manual filing system means something like a **filing cabinet** or **card index**.

In Figure 10.1 below a school is storing information about its students on record cards. These cards are stored in alphabetical order in a box. This is an example of a card-index filing system. Each student has their own card; this is their **record**. On a student's card certain things about the student are recorded like name and date of birth; these individual pieces of information are called **fields**.

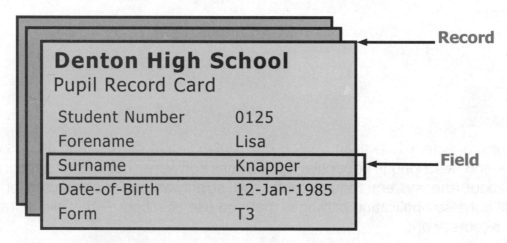

Fig 10.1: Records and fields in a manual filing system.

There are many problems with storing information this way and it was partly because of these problems that computers were invented. The problems associated with manual filing systems are listed below.

- Searching through all of the records to find answers to questions about the information can be very time-consuming. Suppose a health centre kept all of its patient's medical records in filing cabinets and needed a list of all the women who had given birth in the last six months. To get this list someone would have to search through all of the female patients' medical records by hand and look for everyone who had given birth in the last six months. This would be very time consuming and there would be no guarantee that some records would not get overlooked;

- Large manual filing systems take up a lot of space. This can be expensive for businesses and other organisations because they need more office space, which they have to rent or buy. It also costs more to light and heat a large office;
- Paper-based records are easily damaged or mixed up with other papers and lost;
- Records are often put back in the wrong place. This makes it much harder to find them next time they're needed.

Computers are used to store information because they solve all of these problems. A computer-based filing system can store a lot of information in a very small space, search through the information very quickly and produce printed lists and reports about the information very easily.

Files, records and fields

Information in computer-based filing systems is stored in **data files**. A **file** is a collection of **related records**. Related records means that each record in a file will contain the same sort of information as all the other records. A record must have at least one **field.** A field contains one individual item of data.

Figure 10.2 shows part of a file used by a bookshop to store information about the books they are selling. The records are related because each one stores information about a book for sale in the shop.

These are the **fields**
— there are **four** fields in each record of this file.

ISBN is the **key field**. This is the field that has a different value in every record. It is used to distinguish one record from another. Some books could have the same title, author or publisher. The ISBN is the only way a particular book can be picked out.

A key field uniquely identifies an individual record.

ISBN	Title	Author	Publisher
1-23761-121-3	Complete Cat Care	Claudia Heiniken	Stones and Douglas
1-37463-126-4	Build Your Own Boat	Brian Deacon	Taylor & Co
1-26834-217-7	Better Homes	Julia Stone	Taylor & Co
1-86272-341-5	Practical Pottery	Dennis Cooper	NTC International
1-32627-219-3	DIY Welding	Jane Masters	Stones and Douglas

This is one complete **record** — there are **five** records in this file.

Fig 10.2: Records and fields in a computer-based filing system.

Fixed and variable length records

A fixed length record is one where the length of the fields in each record has been set to be a certain maximum number of characters long. Suppose a field that was going to contain a name was set to be 25 characters long. This means that the field could only ever contain up to 25 characters. If all of the fields in the record have a fixed length like this then the record is said to be a **fixed length record**. The problem with fixed length records is that each field very rarely contains the maximum number of characters allowed. This means that a lot of space is needlessly set aside and wasted. Also, values sometimes cannot be entered because they are too large to fit inside the allowed space in a field. The advantage of fixed length records is that they make file processing much easier because the start and end of each record is always a fixed number of characters apart. This makes it much easier to locate both individual records and fields.

A **variable length record** is one where the length of a field can change to allow data of any size to fit. The advantage of variable length records is that space is not wasted, only the space needed is ever used. The main problem with variable length records is that it is much more difficult to locate the start and end of individual records and fields. This is because they are not separated by a fixed amount of characters. To separate variable length records each field has a special character to mark where it ends — called an **end-of-field marker**. When records need to be located the computer must count through the end-of-field markers to locate individual records and fields.

M	r										
D	a	m	o	n							
B	o	l	d								
3	1		P	a	r	k		L	a	n	e

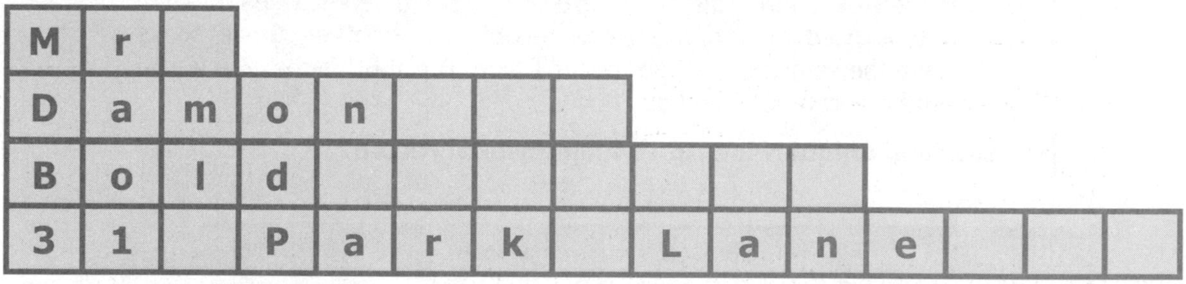

Fig 10.3: Fixed length records
A set amount of storage space is set aside for each field. If the contents of a field don't fill the space completely it is remains empty and is wasted.

M	r	#	D	a	m	o	n	#	B	o	l	d	#
3	1		P	a	r	k		L	a	n	e	#	

Fig 10.4: Variable length records.
A special marker (# in this example) indicates where each field ends. The length of a field depends upon the data that is placed in it. Only the space needed for a field is ever used — so none is wasted.

Computerised databases

A database is a structured collection of related data. It can be a single file that contains a large number of records or a collection of files. Many modern databases are described as being **relational**. This just describes the way that data is organised within the database. A relational database stores data in **tables** that are linked together using common fields.

The example shown in Figure 10.5 shows a relational database for a video rental shop. Information is stored in separate data tables about members, videos and loans. The tables are linked to each other using the video number and member number fields. This makes it possible to use any combination of fields from the three tables. So for example, even though a loan record does not contain the title of the film on loan this can be "looked up" in the videos table using the video number.

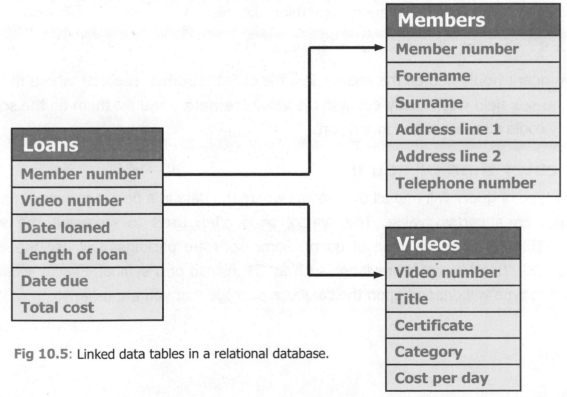

Members
Member number
Forename
Surname
Address line 1
Address line 2
Telephone number

Loans
Member number
Video number
Date loaned
Length of loan
Date due
Total cost

Videos
Video number
Title
Certificate
Category
Cost per day

Fig 10.5: Linked data tables in a relational database.

File operations

File operations are the different things that can be done to a computer file. The main types of file operation are **searching**, **sorting**, **updating** and **merging** — these are all described in more detail on the next few pages.

Searching

Searching, or **interrogating** a file, involves looking for an individual record or group of records that match a certain condition. Searches are also called **queries**. To search a database the user must enter a **query**. The query tells the software which fields to look at in each record and what to look for. Some of the more commonly used types of query are described below.

Exactly equal to

This type of query will find all the records where the data in a field is **exactly equal to** a certain value. The **=** symbol is often used to represent the words EQUAL TO or EQUALS in this type of query. Some software packages do use the words EQUAL TO or EQUALS or an abbreviation such as EQ instead of a symbol. Exactly what you need to type will depend upon the database package that you are using.

E.g. suppose a school wanted to search its student records to find all the female students, they might use a query something like this:

QUERY student_records.sex = "female"

This query would find all the records in a file called **student_records** where the data in the **sex** field was exactly equal to the value **"female"**, and list them on the screen. They could also be printed in a report.

Greater than or equal to

This type of query will find all the records where the data in a field is **greater than or equal to** a certain value. The symbol **>** is often used to represent the words GREATER THAN in this type of query. Some software packages will use the words GREATER THAN or an abbreviation such as GT instead of a symbol. Exactly what you need to type will depend upon the database package that you are using.

E.g. suppose a shop wanted to search its stock records to find all the products that were for sale over a particular price, they might use a query something like this:

QUERY stock_file.price>1.99

This query would find all the records in a file called **stock_file** where the data in the **price** field was **greater than** the value **1.99**

QUERY stock_file.price>=1.99

This query would find all the records in a file called **stock_file** where the data in the **price** field was **greater than** _or_ **equal to** the value **1.99**

Less than or equal to

This type of query will find all the records where the data in a field is **less than or equal to** a certain value. The symbol **<** is often used in this type of query to represent the words LESS THAN. Some software packages will use the words LESS THAN or an abbreviation such as LT instead of a symbol. Exactly what you need to type will depend upon the database package that you are using.

E.g. suppose a second hand car sales company wanted to search its stock records to find all the cars that were for sale under a particular price, they might use a query something like this:

QUERY car_file.price<1500

This query would find all the records in a file called **car_file** where the data in the **price** field was **less than** the value **1500**

QUERY car_file.price<=1500

This query would find all the records in a file called **car_file** where the data in the **price** field was **less than** _or_ **equal to** the value **1500**

Ranges

This type of query will find all the records where the data in one or more fields lies within a range of values.

E.g. suppose a school wanted to search its student records to find all the students with an average examination mark between 30 and 50 percent, they might use a query something like the one shown over the page.

QUERY student_records.average_mark>=30
AND student_records.average_mark<=50

This query would find all the records in a file called **student_records** where the data in the **average_mark** field was **greater than or equal** to the value 30 *and* less **than or equal to** the value **50**

AND

This type of query will find all the records that match two or more search criteria.

E.g. suppose a second hand car sales company wanted to search its stock records to find all the red Ford cars that were for sale, they might use a query something like this:

QUERY car_file.colour="red" AND car_file.manufacturer="Ford"

This query would find all the records in a file called **car_file** where the data in the **colour** field was **exactly equal to** the value "**red**" **AND** where the data in the **manufacturer** field was **exactly equal to** the value "**Ford**".

This type of search finds records that match <u>each one</u> of the search criteria, so in the example above only red Ford cars would be searched for. Red cars made by another manufacturer or different coloured cars made by Ford would not be listed in the results of the query.

OR

This type of query will find all the records that match a choice of different search criteria.

E.g. suppose a school wanted to search its student records to find all the students that were in Year 7 or Year 11, they might use a query something like this:

QUERY student_file.year=7 OR student_file.year=11

This query would find all the records in a file called **student_records** where the data in the **year** field was either **equal to** the value **7 <u>OR</u> equal to** the value **11**.

This type of search finds records that match <u>either one</u> of the search criteria, so in the example above only students in either year 7 or year 11 would be searched for. Students in any other year would not be listed in the results of the query.

NOT

This type of query will find all the records that <u>do not</u> have a particular value in a field. The <> symbol is often used to represent the word NOT in this type of query. Some software packages may use the words NOT or NOT EQUAL instead of a symbol. Exactly what you need to type will depend upon the database package that you are using.

E.g. suppose a second hand car sales company wanted to search its stock records to find all the cars for sale that weren't blue.

QUERY car_file.colour<>"blue"

This query would find all the records in a file called **car_file** where the data in the **colour** field does not contain the value "**blue**".

This type of search finds records where the data in a specified field <u>does not</u> contain a certain value.

Sorting

Sorting involves putting the records in a file into a particular order, such as alphabetical order. In a student file, for example, a list of all the students in a particular form might need to be printed out in alphabetical order of student name.

Merging

Merging involves combining two files to produce one new file. This can be done by merging a file of new records to be added with another file that contains all of the existing records — called the **master file**.

Updating

The information stored in computer files must be kept up-to-date or it will cause problems for the business or organisation that is using it. Keeping the information in a file up-to-date involves adding new records when they're needed, deleting records that aren't needed and altering the information in a record when it changes. Suppose a mail order company wanted to send out a new catalogue to all of its customers. If its customer records file wasn't up-to-date catalogues could be sent to the wrong addresses. This would cost the company a lot of money in lost catalogues and business. To keep a file up-to-date it must be regularly updated. This involves **inserting**, **deleting** and **amending** records.

Insertion

When a new record needs to be added to a file, it is **inserted**. In a student records file, for example, a new record would need to be inserted when a new student joined the school.

Deletion

Records are **deleted** when they are no longer needed. In a student records file, for example, a record would need to be deleted when a student left the school.

Amendment

Records are **amended**, or changed, when the data in one or more of the fields needs to be altered for some reason. In a student records file, for example, a record would need to be amended when a student moved house and their address changed.

Details of all the changes that need to be made to a master file are often collected together in a **transaction file**. The master file is updated by comparing it with the transaction file and making changes to any records that appear in both files. Normally at least three 'generations' of a master file are kept for backup purposes. If the latest version of the master file is damaged it can be recreated by re-running the previous update using the old master and transaction files.

This method of updating is known as the **grandfather-father-son** method which is illustrated in Figure 10.6 below.

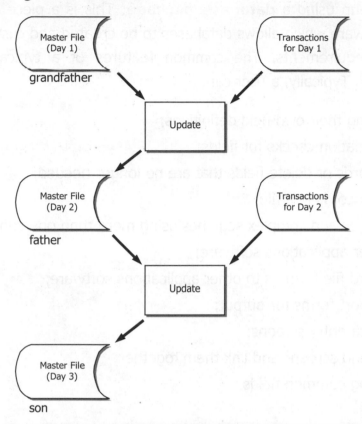

Fig 10.6: The grandfather-father-son method of updating.

Backing up on-line databases

An on-line database is constantly being updated. To make sure no data is lost in the event of hardware failure, special back-up methods are used. **Transaction logging** and **RAID (Redundant Array of Inexpensive Disks)** are two commonly used methods.

Transaction logging involves storing the details of each update in a **transaction log file**. A 'before' and 'after' image of each updated record is also saved. If any part of the database is destroyed an up-to-date copy can be recreated by a utility program using the transaction log file and the 'before' and 'after' images of the updated records.

RAID involves keeping several copies of a database on different disks at the same time. Whenever a record is updated the same changes are made to each copy of the database. This is so that if one disk fails the data will still be safe on the others.

Database packages

Most databases are set-up using a **database package**. This is a piece of general-purpose application software which allows databases to be created and customised to meet a user's exact requirements. The common features of a typical database package are listed below. Typically, a user can:

- create a file by entering their own field definitions;
- specify automatic validation checks for fields;
- add new fields to records or delete fields that are no longer needed;
- add, edit and delete records in a file;
- perform simple searches and complex searches using more than one condition;
- import data from other applications software;
- export data in standard file formats to other applications software;
- create customised report forms for output;
- create customised data entry screens;
- create customised menu screens and link them together;
- link files together using common fields.

Fig 10.7: MS Access — a popular database package.

Questions

1. The table below shows part of a computer file used by a video shop to store information about its stock.

Title	Artist	Format	Status
Unhinged Melody	Roy & Jeremy	CD Single	In stock
Bounce	Nightshade	CD Album	Out of stock
Unhinged Melody	Terrance Tone	CD Single	In stock
Easy Street	The Vagabonds	CD Single	In stock
A Whiter Shade of Grey	Cliff Pilchard	CD Single	Out of stock
Greatest Hits III	David O'Connell	CD Album	In stock

(a) How many **records** are shown in the table? (1)

(b) How many **fields** are there in each record? (1)

(c) What **data** is stored in the **third field** of the **fifth record**? (1)

(d) What **data** is stored in the **first field** of the **second record**? (1)

(e) What does the term **key field** mean? (2)

(f) Suggest a new field that could be added to each record and used as the **key field**. (1)

2. A library uses a computer system to store details of books and members. The system is also used to store details of the books each member has on loan.

(a) Describe **two** tasks, which the librarian could carry out more easily with this system than with a manual system. (2)

(b) The members file contains these fields:

> Member number
> Surname
> Other names
> Address
> Post Code

(i) Which field must have different contents in every record? (1)

(ii) What is this type of field called? (1)

NEAB 1996 Paper 2 Tier P

3. A very large multi-screen cinema uses a database system to help with its seat booking system. Part of the database it uses is shown below.

Screen	Film	Certificate	Seats still available	Adult ticket	Child ticket	Late night showing	Morning showing
1	Dumbo	U	50	£3.50	£2.50	No	Yes
2	Superman V	PG	40	£40	£3	No	Yes
3	Evil Dead Part 4	18	35	£4	Not available	Yes	No
4	Rocky Horror Show	18	20	£5	Not available	No	No
5	X-men	12	5	£4	£3	No	No
6	Never Ending Story	U	-10	£4	£2.50	No	Yes

Only some of the records and fields are shown.

(a) The database contains two mistakes. Say what each mistake is, and give a reason why you think it is a mistake. (4)

(b) In order to search the database, the following commands are used.

List
For
Equals
Greater than
Less than
And
Or

For example, to get a list of the screens and films where there is a morning showing you would type:

List Screen, Film **For** Morning showing **Equals** Yes

(i) Complete the line below to show what you would type to get a list of the screens and films which have a certificate of 18.

List ...., ... **For** .... (3)

(ii) Now write the instructions needed to produce a list of films and certificates that have more than 20 seats available and have a late night showing. (4)

NEAB 2000 Paper 1 Tier H

4. A ladies' fashion catalogue uses a database for stock control. Part of the stock database is shown below.

Catalogue N°	Size	Colour	Pattern	Price
1000345	12	Pink	Floral	27.99
1000347	12	Blue	Plain	29.50
1000429	14	Yellow	Plain	29.50
1000438	16	Red	Floral	39.99
1000513	14	Pink	Stripe	34.99
1000516	14	Red	Plain	41.75

(a) Which field would be the best to use as the **key field** ? (1)

(b) Suggest **two** other fields that would need to be included in each stock record before the database file can be used for **stock control**. (2)

(c) Explain briefly how these two fields can be used to maintain stock levels in the catalogue company's warehouse. (3)

5. A pupil database contains two data files. The structure of the two files is shown below.

Pupils
Pupil number
Surname
Forename
Date of Birth
Address 1
Address 2
Address 3
Contact phone number
Home phone number
Subject code 1
Subject code 2
Subject code 3
Subject code 4
Form

Subjects
Subject code
Subject name

(a) Why is it better to store the data in two separate files, rather than keeping it all in one file. (1)

(b) Why is Date of Birth stored rather than age? (1)

(c) To find all the pupils in the same form a search can be carried out. In this database package searches take the form:

<fieldname> <comparison><value>

a search for surname = "Robinson " would find all pupils with the surname Robinson.

Write down the search you would carry out to find all the pupils in the Form called 7B. (3)

(d) The headteacher wants to be able to send personalised letters to the pupils' parent or guardian.

What extra field would be needed to allow the letters to be produced? (1)

NEAB 1998 Paper 2 Tier F

Websites

Visit the websites of the publishers of the database packages listed below to find out more about their products.

- **Microsoft Access** at **www.microsoft.com/access/**
- **Lotus Approach** at **www.lotus.com**
- **Claris FileMaker Pro** at **www.claris.com**
- **Oracle** at **www.oracle.com**
- **IBM DB2** at **www.software.ibm.com/data/db2/udb**

Chapter 11

A **spreadsheet package** is a general purpose computer package that is designed to perform **calculations**. A spreadsheet is a table which is divided into **rows** and **columns**. Columns have a letter at the top and rows have a number at the side. Lines divide the rows and columns up into boxes called **cells**. The parts of a spreadsheet are shown in Figure 11.1. A cell can contain **text**, a **number** or a **formula**. Individual cells are identified by their **cell reference number** which normally contains a column letter and a row number.

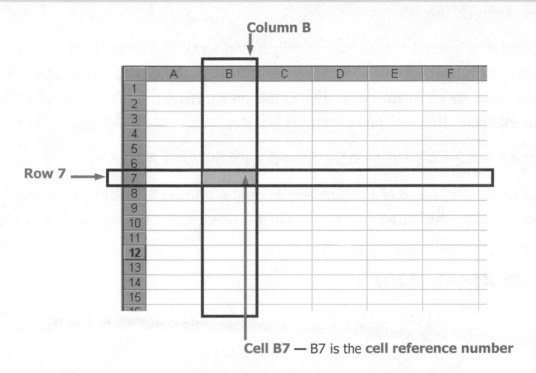

Cell B7 — B7 is the **cell reference number**

Fig 11.1: The parts of a spreadsheet

Using a formula

A **formula** is used on a spreadsheet to perform a calculation using the numbers in other cells. The result of the calculation is displayed in the cell where the formula has been entered.

A simple formula can be used to add, subtract, multiply or divide numbers. To carry out these sorts of calculation the symbols below are used in a formula:

+   to **add**

-      to **subtract**

*   to **multiply**

/   to **divide**

Suppose, for example, that you wanted to add two numbers on a spreadsheet together. If the numbers were in cells **A1** and **A2** the formula that you would need to enter would be something like this:

= A1+A2

You would need to enter this formula in the cell where you wanted the answer to appear. The "=" sign at the beginning of the formula is there to tell the spreadsheet package that what's been entered is a formula. Some spreadsheet packages use a different symbol to do this.

To make it easier to enter a longer, more complicated formula, spreadsheet packages also have special **mathematical functions** built-in. Two of the most commonly used functions are used to calculate either the **SUM** or **AVERAGE** of a range of cells. Suppose, for example, that you had a formula like this:

=A1+A2+A3+A4+A5+A6+A7+A8+A9+A10

This formula would add up all of the numbers in cells **A1** to **A10**. Instead of typing in such a long formula, the **SUM** function could be used. On most spreadsheets the formula would be something like this:

= SUM (A1: A10)

If a number of cells need the same formula it can be copied and pasted in the same way as text.

Similarly, to work out the average of the numbers in cells **A1** to **A10**, the **AVERAGE** function could be used. On most spreadsheets the formula would be something like this:

= AVERAGE (A1: A10)

Exactly what you need to type in will depend upon the spreadsheet package that you are using.

Cell formats

Spreadsheet packages, like word processing packages, have built-in formatting options which allow you to change the way a spreadsheet looks. Anything that affects the appearance of a cell is called a **cell format**. Some of the more commonly used **cell formatting** options are described below. These are all features which any good spreadsheet package should have included.

Changing font size and style

The style of text in a cell can be changed. Different styles of text are called **fonts** (there's more about this in the next chapter). The size of text in individual cells or groups of cells can be changed. In most spreadsheet packages **bold**, *italic* and <u>underlined</u> and different coloured text can also be used.

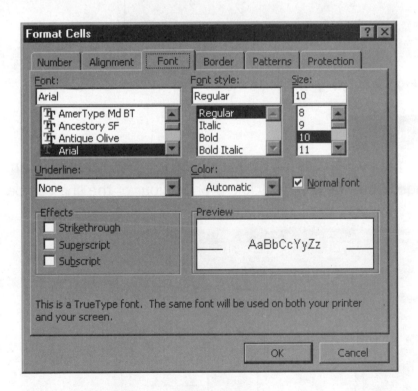

Fig 11.2: Changing font style and size

Changing text alignment

The position of text in a cell can be changed using **text alignment** formats. Text can be aligned **vertically** or **horizontally**. **Justification** is a type of horizontal alignment. The contents of a cell can be justified **left**, **right**, or in the **centre**.

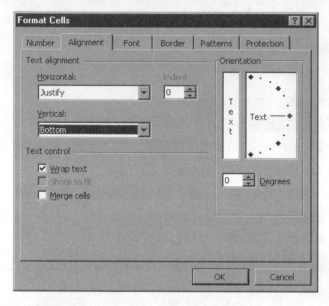

Fig 11.3: Changing the alignment of text

Borders and lines

Individual cells or groups of cells can have borders drawn around them. In most spreadsheet packages both the style, thickness and colour of the line can be changed.

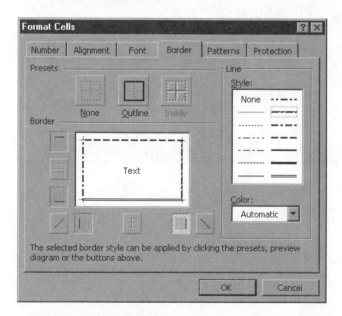

Fig 11.4: Putting a border around cells

Inserting extra rows and columns

Sometimes, when working on a spreadsheet, it becomes necessary to insert an extra row or an extra column. Most spreadsheets allow you to do this quite easily. When an extra row or column is inserted the spreadsheet automatically updates the cell references in any formulas that are affected by the change.

Changing column width and row height

The size of a cell depends upon the width of the column that it is in and the height of the row that it is in. When any spreadsheet is being set up for the first time all of the columns and rows have the same width and height, which means that all the cells are the same size. At this stage the size of the cells is said to be set to the **default value**. When data is entered into a cell it might not fit into the size allowed by the default value. If this is the case the column width can be adjusted by the user until the data fits in the cell. Similarly, if a row is too narrow (or too high), its height can be altered by the user. Some spreadsheets can be set up to automatically adjust the column width when data is entered. Such an option is normally called **'best-fit'** or **'auto-size'**.

The height of Row 1 has been increased

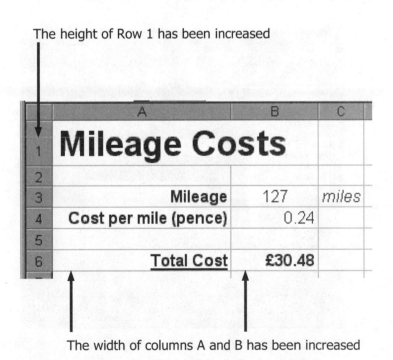

The width of columns A and B has been increased

Fig 11.5: Changing column width and row height

Data formats

Anything that affects the appearance of numbers in a cell is called a **data format**. Some of the more commonly used data format options are described below. These are all features that any good spreadsheet package should have.

Decimal

Decimal data format is used when a number needs a decimal point in it. When using decimal format the required number of decimal places must be chosen by the user. For example to display two decimal places after the decimal point, the data format would be '**0.00**' or '**#.##**' depending upon the particular spreadsheet package that is being used.

Currency

A lot of spreadsheets are used for financial calculations. Currency format is used to display a **£** or **$** symbol in front of a number. The required number of decimal places (normally 2 or 0) can be specified in the currency format.

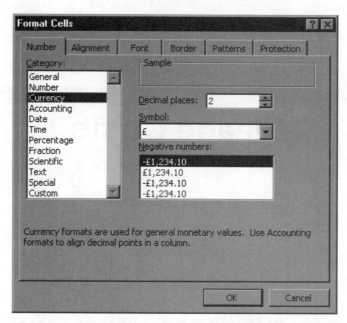

Fig 11.6: Specifying a currency format of 2 decimal places

Date

Date format is used in cells where dates have been entered to specify the way that the date should be displayed.

E.g. A date format of **dd-mm-yy**, would display the date **12th June 2001** as **12-06-01**, whereas a date format of **dd-mmm-yyyy**, would display the same date as **12-Jun-2001**.

Sorting data

One very useful feature of a spreadsheet package is the **sort** facility. This allows the columns or rows of a spreadsheet to be sorted into **alphabetical** or **numerical** order of a value in a particular row or column.

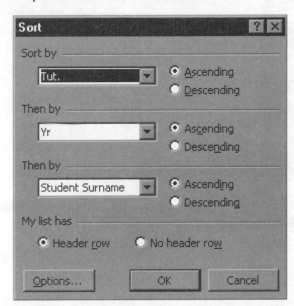

Fig 11.7: Data can be sorted quickly on a spreadsheet

Graphs and charts

Most spreadsheet packages include facilities for representing information in the form of a graph or chart. The more common types of charts and graphs that are used are **bar charts**, **pie charts** and **line graphs**. A **chart wizard** gives step-by-step help when drawing a graph or chart — an example of this is shown in Figure 11.8.

The first step in creating a graph or chart is to enter the data on the spreadsheet.

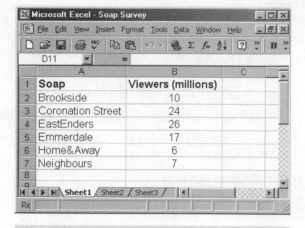

The next step is to choose the type of chart or graph. A **chart wizard** can be used to help with this.

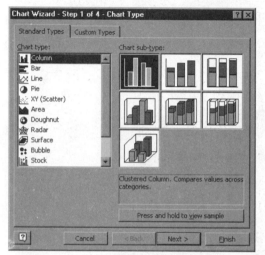

The graph is automatically drawn by the spreadsheet software. It can then be copied and pasted into other applications if required.

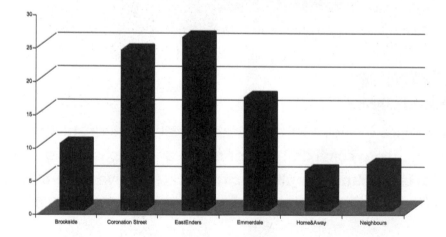

Fig 11.8: Using a spreadsheet to draw a graph

Questions

1. Describe how the **cell** and **data formatting** features of a spreadsheet can be used to solve the problems listed below when a new spreadsheet is being set-up.

    (a)   The text is too wide for the cell it is in.   (1)

    (b)   The numbers in a column need to be displayed with two decimal
          places.   (1)

    (c)   Some of the numbers need a pound (£) sign.   (1)

    (d)   The column headings need to stand out more.   (1)

    (e)   The numbers in a column need to be added up to give a total.   (1)

2. You have been asked to plan a friend's birthday party. To help investigate the cost of the party you have set up the spreadsheet shown below.

	A	B	C
1	**Number of Guests**	60	
2			
3	**Item**		**Cost**
4	Room Hire		£100
5	Buffet (per person)	£3.25	£195
6	Disco		£150
7		**Total Cost**	**£445**

    (a)   Write down the **address** of the **cell** that contains the cost of room hire. (1)

    (b)   Write down the **formula** that would be entered in cell **C5**.   (1)

    (c)   Write down the **formula** that would be entered in cell **C7**.   (1)

    (d)   You have decided to investigate the effects of changing the number
          of guests. Write down the **address** of the **cell** whose contents
          will need to be changed.   (1)

    (e)   Changing the number in this cell would also cause the numbers
          in **two** other cells to change. Write down the **addresses** of
          these **cells**.   (1)

    (f)   What **data format** has been used for the **Cost** column ?   (1)

    (g)   What **data format** has been used in cell **B5** ?   (1)

3. (a) Describe the **cell** and **data formatting** features that have been used in the spreadsheet shown below. (10)

	A	B	C	D	E	F	G
1	Supermarket Price Comparison						
2							
3		BACON	BREAD	CHEESE	EGGS	MILK	
4	Product Size	425g	Medium Loaf	425g	Dozen	1 Pint	
5							Total Cost
6	Bettabuys	1.98	0.65	2.25	1.09	0.35	£6.32
7	Cheapco	2.27	0.62	2.62	1.21	0.32	£7.04
8	SuperSaver	2.09	0.61	2.18	1.05	0.34	£6.27
9							
10	Average Cost	£2.11	£0.63	£2.35	£1.12	£0.34	£6.54
11							

(b) Write down the formula that has been used to calculate the value shown in cell B10. (2)

(c) Write down the formula that has been used to calculate the value shown in cell G6. (2)

4. A group of friends who live in the North East of England regularly go to pop concerts. Next year they are planning to go to five concerts. Not everyone wants to go to all of the concerts. Below is part of the spreadsheet that is used to work out the cost for each trip. This is produced once it is known how many people will be going to each concert and the cost of the tickets.

	A	B	C	D	E	F	G
1	Group	Venue	Travel costs	No. of	Travel costs	Cost of 1	Total cost
2			for car	people in	for 1 person	concert	of trip for
3				the car		ticket	one person
4							
5	Oasis	London	£60.00	4	£15.00	£20.00	£35.00
6	Spice girls	Birmingham	£40.00	4	£10.00	£18.00	£28.00
7	Blur	Newcastle	£15.00	3	£5.00	£17.00	£22.00
8	Hanson	Manchester	£30.00	2	£15.00	£15.00	£30.00
9	Peter Andre	Glasgow	£40.00	2	£20.00	£15.00	£35.00

(a) The travel cost for the trip to Manchester was wrongly entered. The cost should have been **£35 not £30**. Which **cell** must be changed? (1)

(b) Which **two other cells** would change automatically as a result of this change? (2)

(c) What **formula** would be in the cell E5? (1)

(d) Name **one** other cell, in another column, that contains a **different** formula. (1)

(e) Last year the friends used a calculator to work out their costs.

Give **three advantages** of using a spreadsheet like the one given above, compared with their old manual method. (3)

NEAB 1998 Paper 1 Tier F

5. Paula Wilkinson has decided to use a spreadsheet to help her investigate the costs of redecorating and purchasing new furniture for her bedroom. You can see one particular plan on the spreadsheet below.

	A	B	C	D	E
1	**Item**	**Unit cost**	**Unit**	**Quantity**	**Total cost**
2		**(£)**		**needed**	**of item (£)**
3	Paint		Litre		
4	Wallpaper		Roll		
5	Bed				
6	Wardrobe				
7	Desk				
8	TV				
9	Carpet Tiles		Tile		
10	Curtains		Pair		
11					
12				**Total cost**	
13					
14				**Amount available**	
15					
16				**Balance left**	

(a) State the formula which would be contained in the following cells:

    (i)   E3

    (ii) E12

    (iii) E16   (3)

(b) What data format should be used for the unit cost and total cost of item columns?   (1)

(c) State a method of inserting the formula needed in cells E4 to E10 other than typing each one in separately.   (1)

(d) Formulae and data formats are two items Paula would need to consider when designing this spreadsheet. State **five** other items which she would also need to take into account.   (5)

NEAB 1996 Paper 1 Tier Q

Websites

- Visit the PC World website at **www.pcworld.com/heres_how/** and follow the link to spreadsheets for some useful tips on getting the most out of spreadsheet software.

- For tips and information on how to create a well-designed spreadsheet visit **www.melbpc.org.au/pcupdate/9409/409sset.htm**

- If you use Microsoft Excel resources and information can be found at **www.microsoft.com/office/excel/**

Chapter 12

A word processor can be used to **write**, **edit**, **format** and **print** text. Before word processors, printed documents were typed directly on to the paper using manual typewriters (Figure 12.1). The main problem with using typewriters was that if a mistake was made it could not be corrected without leaving any trace. Often, if a typist made a mistake, the entire document would have to be typed out again. This made the process of producing printed documents very slow and time-consuming.

Word processing software was developed to overcome these problems. All word processing packages have many special features in common, which can be used to improve both the appearance and quality of printed text. The common features of word processing packages are described in this chapter.

Fig 12.1: A manual typewriter

Common functions of word processors

Font size

This function allows the size of any part of the text to be changed. The font size is changed by changing its **point size**. The larger the point size, the bigger the text will be.

This text is **12 point** size.

This text is **18 point** size.

Font style

This option allows the style of any part of the text to be changed. The font styles that are available will depend on the word processor that you are using. Each different font style has its own special name. Some examples of different types of font are shown below.

This font is called Broadway

This font is called Bookman Old Style

This font is called Ravie

Bold, *italic* and underline

Other effects that can be used to change the appearance of text are options to make it **bold**, *italic* or underlined (*or* any combination of these).

Word processing packages often collect similar functions like these together on a '**toolbar**' to make them easier to use. The '**formatting toolbar**' of a popular word typical processing package is shown in Figure 12.2 below.

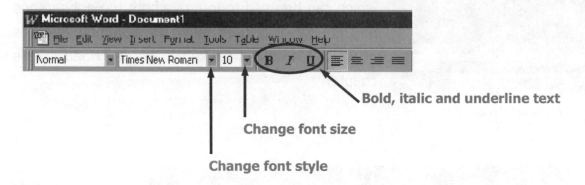

Fig 12.2: The formatting toolbar of a typical word processing package

Cut, copy and paste

The **cut** facility of a word processor allows you to choose a part of your text and 'cut it out'. 'Cut' text can either be thrown away or '**pasted**' back onto the page in another place. The **copy** facility allows you to choose part of your text and then paste a copy of it elsewhere in your document. The cut, copy and paste facilities of a word processor will also allow you to work with graphics in the same way as with text.

Tabulation

Tabulation allows the tab key 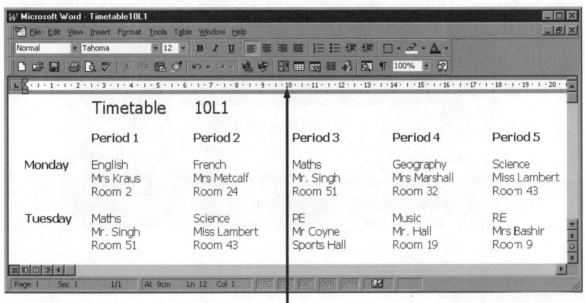 to be set to jump forward a pre-set distance across the page each time it is pressed. The user can set up the distance that the tab key will jump to any value they want. The text in Figure 12.3 below has been arranged in columns using tabs. All of the text in each column is lined up with a tab stop along the ruler line.

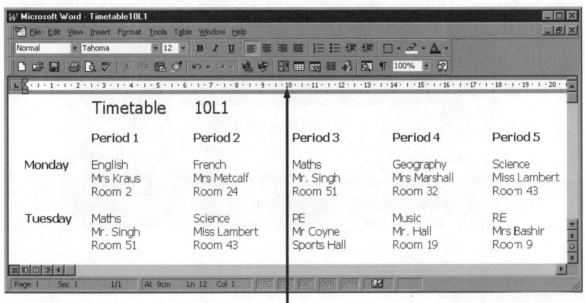

Fig 12.3: Using 'tabs' to align text

Text in this column is lined up at the tab stop which is at 10 cm on the ruler line.

Word-wrap

Word-wrap means that when you are typing you do not have to press the enter key ↵ at the end of a line; the word processor will begin a new line whenever one is needed. The enter key is only pressed to start a new paragraph or to leave a deliberate gap of one or more lines between blocks of text.

Find and replace

Search and replace allows you to tell the word processor to look for one word and replace it with another. This can be done **selectively** for just part of a document or **globally**. Selective search and replace will check each time it finds the search word whether or not you want it replacing. Global search and replace just finds every occurrence of the search word and replaces it without asking first. In the example shown in Figure 12.4 below the user wants the word 'Chalk' replaced by the word 'Cheese'

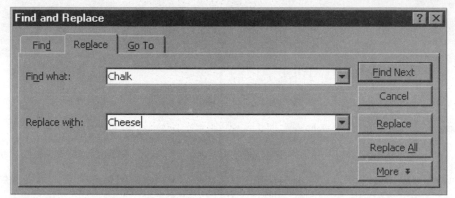

Fig 12.4: Using 'find and replace'.

Line spacing

Line spacing is used to change the amount of space between lines of text. Normal text is single spaced. Figure 12.5 below shows the line spacing options available in a typical word processing package — such as 'single', '1.5 times', and 'double'.

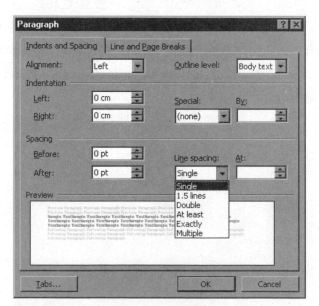

Fig 12.5: Changing line spacing.

You can also change the space between lines by adjusting the 'leading'. This term originates from the days when typesetters placed stripes of lead (metal) between lines of text created from individual metal letters. The finished plate was then inked and used to print books and newspapers. The lines in this block of text are **'double spaced'**.

Spell checkers

A **spell checker** uses a built-in dictionary to check the spellings in your text. When a spell checker finds words that are unknown, it will offer possible alternatives from its dictionary and ask if you want to choose a replacement, delete the unknown word completely, keep the word as it is, or enter your own alternative word. Spell checkers are not foolproof, however, and you do need to have a reasonable knowledge of correct spellings, otherwise you might end up choosing incorrect alternative words as corrections, making your finished text read very strangely indeed. Figure 12.6 below shows a spell check facility being used. The dialogue box shows incorrect spellings and suggests possible words to use as corrections.

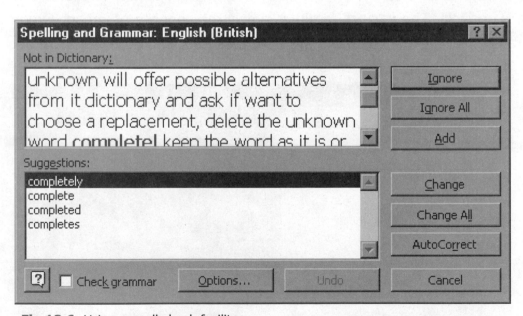

Fig 12.6: Using a spell check facility.

Grammar checkers

A **grammar checker** uses a built in set of 'rules' about the grammar of the language that you are using. Grammar checkers <u>**do not**</u> check spellings, they just check that what you have written follows the rules of a language correctly.

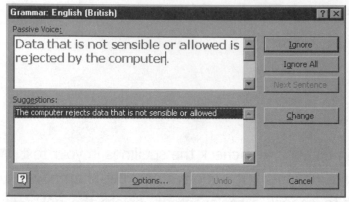

Fig 12.7: Using a grammar check facility.

Importing and exporting

One of the major advantages that modern word processors have over typewriters is that they allow you to import graphics and combine graphics with text. What this means is that diagrams and pictures produced using other software packages can be included on the page along with your text. The **import** facility is the feature which makes this possible. The **export** facility is simply the opposite of import. Export allows you to transfer work produced using the word processor into other software packages.

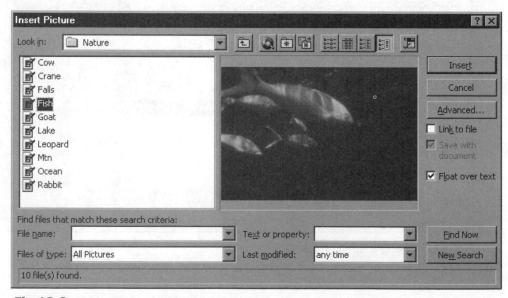

Fig 12.8: Using an import facility.

Justification

Justification is a feature which adds extra spaces to a block of text to line it up in a particular way. Text can be **left justified**, **right justified**, **centred** or **fully justified**. The examples below show you what these different sorts of justification look like.

The text opposite is **left justified**. This means that each line of text is lined up on the left hand side only.

"It was the best of times, it was the worst of times, it was the age of wisdom, it was the age of foolishness, it was the epoch of belief, it was the epoch of incredulity, it was the season of Light,

The text opposite is **fully justified**. This means that each line of text is lined up on both the left and right hand sides.

it was the season before of Darkness, it was the spring of hope, it was the winter of despair, we had everything before us, we had nothing before us, we were all going direct to heaven, we were all going direct the other way

The text opposite is **centred**. This means that each line of text is lined up in the centre of the page.

— in short, the period was so far like the present period, that some of its noisiest authorities insisted on its being received, for good or for evil, in the superlative degree of comparison only."

The text opposite is **right aligned**. This means that each line of text is lined up on the right hand side only.

A Tale of Two Cities
By Charles Dickens

Mail Merging

Mail merging is a special feature that is included in most modern word processing packages. It allows the user to create a **standard letter** and then merge it with data from a spreadsheet, database or other text file. This file is called the **source data file**. During the merging process data from fields in individual records in the source data file is inserted into spaces that have been specially marked in the standard letter. So a 'personalised' letter is produced for each record in the source data file. This process is illustrated below in Figure 12.9. Mail merging is a very quick method of producing letters which each contain virtually the same information except for the names and addresses of the people in each letter. Only one standard letter has to be written in order to produce many mail-merged copies. This is how many businesses send out junk mail to people.

A source data file is either prepared or imported from an existing file.

Title	Forename	Surname	Address 1	Address 2	Address 3	Postcode
Mr.	Stephen	Davidson	31 Cornwallis Road	Boxford	Turnbridge	TB19 2XZ
Mr.	Peter	Dewhurst	12 Lilac Grove	Hall Grange	Turnbridge	TB17 6EX
Mrs.	Juila	Grafton	31 Shelbourne Road	Brampton	Turnbridge	TB12 7TB
Miss	Betty	Grant	19 Hall Drive	Evesham	Rockwell	RW9 14XT
Ms	Anthony	Howarth	34 Peel Street	Evesham	Rockwell	RW2 12BQ

A standard letter is written and 'markers' are placed in it to indicate where data from the source data file is to be inserted into each individual letter.

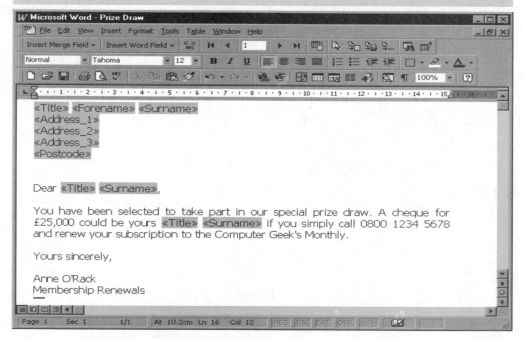

Fig 12.9: Producing mail merged letters.

The standard letter is merged with data from the source data file to produce individual letters.

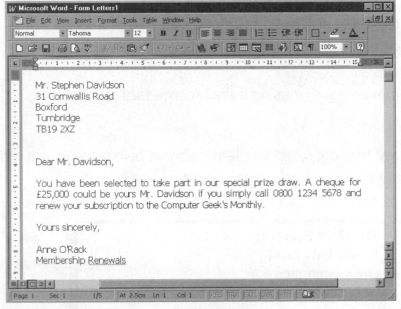

Advantages of word processors

Using a word processor to produce printed text has many advantages when compared with older manual methods such as using a typewriter. The main advantages of word processors are: -

- Mistakes can be corrected easily without leaving any trace;
- Much better presentation of text is possible with formatting features such as different font styles and sizes, coloured text and justification;
- Text can be easily inserted, deleted or rearranged without having to start again;
- Documents can be saved on disk and used again whenever necessary;
- Pictures, graphs, tables and charts can be easily included alongside text;
- Multiple copies of the same document can be easily produced;
- Standard letters can be mass-produced very quickly using mail merge;
- Documents can be transferred instantly anywhere in the world via electronic communications links;
- Spelling and grammar can be checked automatically;
- Many desk top publishing (DTP) facilities such as inserting clipart and arranging text in columns are now available in word processing packages — these are described in the next chapter.

Questions

1. Mail merge is a feature that is included with most word processing packages.

   (a) Describe the steps involved in carrying out a **mail merge**.   (3)

   (b) Describe **one** possible way that a business could use a mail merge facility.   (1)

   (c) Give **two** advantages of using a mail merge facility.   (2)

2. A school secretary has prepared the letter shown below using a word processing package on one of the computers in the office.

   The Dene Schook
   Woodlands Road
   Great Grampton
   GG1 2WT

   Tel: (01725) 263547

   Dear Parents,
   As we look forward to Christmad and the end of the autumn term, I am pleased to announce that our annual Chritmas Concert will be taking place on Thursday 12th December. Tickets for this event are free but nubers are strictly limited. If you would like to come to the concert tickets can be picked up from the school office. I look forward to seeing you at the concert.

   Yourd sincerely,
   Mrs E. Hicks
   Head Teachr

   (a) Describe **three** improvements that could be made to the letter and the features of the word processing package that should be used to make them.   (6)

   (b) Give **three** advantages of producing the poster using a word processing package rather than a manual typewriter.   (3)

3. A word processing package has been used to change Menu A to Menu B. Give **five** changes that have been carried out. One has been done for you.

Menu A

```
Menu for Today
Starters
Tomato Soup 35p
Melon 60p
Main Courses
Pasta bake £1.00
Fish, chips and peas £1.75
Tuna salad £1.50
Chicken curry and rice £1.75
Sweets
Rhubarb crumble 80p
Fresh fruit salad 80p
```

Menu B

```
            Menu for Today
Starters
        Tomato Soup          35p
        Melon                60p
Main Courses
        Pasta bake           £1.00
        Fish, chips and peas £1.75
        Tuna salad           £1.50
        Chicken curry and rice £1.75
Sweets
        Rhubarb crumble      80p
        Fresh fruit salad    80p
```

Example: Italics used for the different courses.   (5)

NEAB 1999 Paper 2 Tier F

4. You have a friend who wants to buy a word processing package. He has asked for your advice. Assume that all word processing packages will allow you to enter, edit, save and print text and change margins.

Give **four** other features your friend might need in his new word processing package. Explain why he might need each of the features.   (8)

NEAB 1999 Paper 2 Tier F

Websites

- Look up definitions of the key words highlighted in this chapter using the free on-line dictionary of computing at **http://wombat.doc.ic.ac.uk/foldoc/**

- Visit the PC World website at **www.pcworld.com/heres_how/** and follow the link to word processors for some useful tips on getting the most out of word processing software.

- Visit **www.mavisbeacon.com** and use the information there to write a short article about the history of typing — include something about the health risks associated with doing too much typing.

- If you use Microsoft Word resources and information can be found at **www.microsoft.com/office/word**

Chapter 13 — Desk Top Publishing

Desk top publishing, or **DTP** for short, is the use of a **desk top publishing package** on a computer to produce publications such as newspapers, newsletters, magazines, reports and books instead of going through the traditional publishing process. The DTP process is mainly concerned with designing the layout of the pages in a publication. The contents have usually already been prepared, using a word processing package for text and a graphics package for pictures, diagrams and other illustrations. Individual page contents are imported into the desktop publishing package, which is used to organise their layout and appearance.

The parts of a DTP system

To work efficiently with DTP software a high-specification computer with a large amount of RAM and a fast processor is required. This is so that changes can be made to a publication and their effect seen straight away without having to wait for the computer to deal with the many thousands of instructions and calculations that this type of work generates.

The files produced using DTP software contain both graphics and text and can be quite large so a high-capacity hard disk drive is needed to store them. It is also a good idea for a DTP system to have a zip drive, which allows large files to be more easily transferred between computers.

DTP software displays publications in **WYSIWYG** format — which stands for "What you see is what you get". A high-resolution monitor with a large screen is the best type to use for this type of application so that you can actually see what you're getting without straining your eyes.

Another essential piece of hardware for any DTP system is a scanner, which is used to include any hand-drawn or printed graphics that are not already in a digital format within a publication. To ensure that finished publications are of a high standard the scanner should be able to scan high-resolution images.

To output completed publications a high-quality printer is needed such as a laser printer or high-specification inkjet printer. A colour laser printer will give the best quality output but is also the most expensive option.

A typical desk top publishing system is shown below in Figure 13.1.

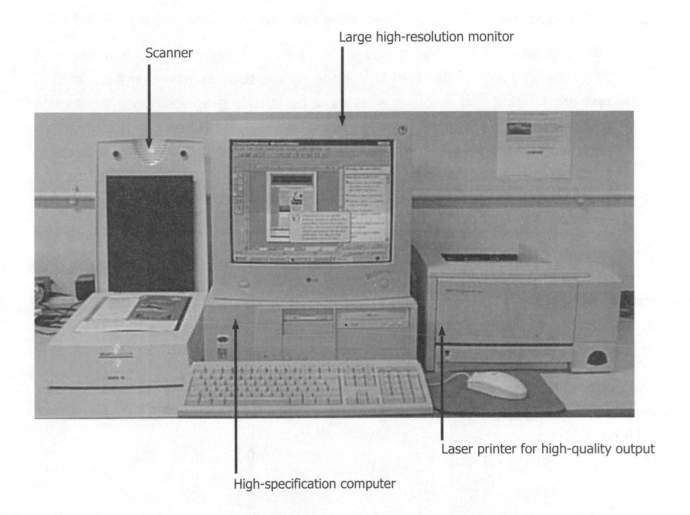

Scanner

Large high-resolution monitor

Laser printer for high-quality output

High-specification computer

Fig 13.1: A desk top publishing (DTP) system.

The stages of desk top publishing

1. The contents of the publication are prepared first.
   - Text is prepared using a word processing package and checked for any mistakes using the spell check facility.
   - Graphics are prepared using a graphics package to create images 'from scratch' or 'tidy up' images from other sources such as: -
     - Graphics captured using a scanner or digital camera;
     - Graphs or charts created from a spreadsheet table;
     - Images from a clipart library;
     - Images downloaded or copied from websites.

2. The general layout of the pages is designed and **templates** are created. A template defines the standard layout for a page such as how many columns of text are needed and where spaces must be left for graphics. Once a template has been set up it can be used to create as many individual pages as required each with the same basic layout. This greatly reduces the time that it takes to organise the layout of each page. Figure 13.2 shows a page template that has been created for a newsletter.

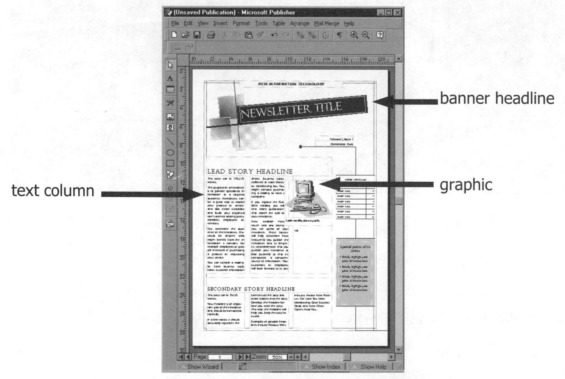

Fig 13.2: A template for a new publication.

3. The text and graphics are imported and put into place.

*   If text doesn't fit on a page it can be automatically 'overflowed' onto the next page. In some DTP applications text is placed inside rectangular boxes called **'frames'**. Frames can have their size adjusted and be linked together if text doesn't fit. Figure 13.3 shows a text frame into which a text file is about to be imported.

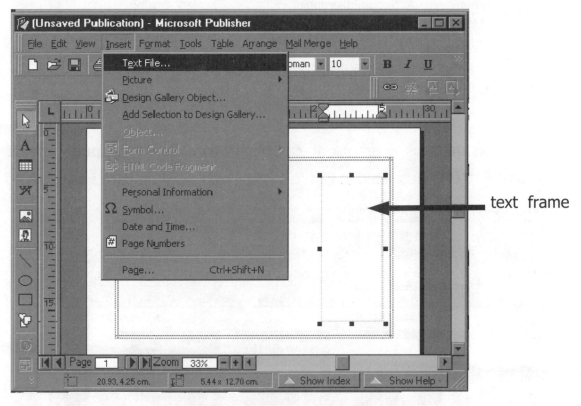

Fig 13.3: Importing text into a text frame.

*   When graphics are put into place most DTP packages will automatically place each one in its own frame. DTP packages that place text and graphics in frames are said to be **'frame-based'**. Microsoft Publisher is an example of a frame-based DTP package. Graphics often need to have their size altered to fit in the space available — **'cropping'** and **'scaling'** are two ways of doing this. Figure 13.4 over the page shows a graphic that has been cropped and scaled.

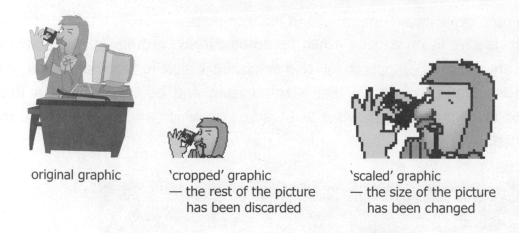

original graphic

'cropped' graphic
— the rest of the picture
has been discarded

'scaled' graphic
— the size of the picture
has been changed

Fig 13.4: Cropping and scaling.

- When text overlaps a graphic it can be **'flowed'** or **'wrapped'** around the graphic — this is illustrated in Figure 13.5 below.

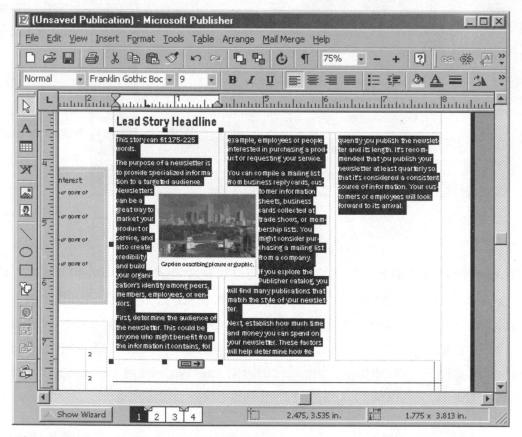

Fig 13.5: Wrapping text around a graphic.

4. Once the layout has been finalised the completed publication is printed and 'proof read' to check for any errors. Any necessary corrections or changes to the layout can then be made. After this a final high quality 'master copy' can be printed using a laser printer. This master copy can be used to make further copies on a photocopying machine. Alternatively the file can be sent to a professional printing company using e-mail or through the conventional post by saving it on disk.

Common features of DTP packages

- ## Fonts

    A good DTP package will include a large variety of fonts which can be whatever size the user requires.

- ## Styles

    Styles allow the user to define the font style, size and colour of text. Once a style has been defined it can be applied to any part of the text whenever necessary. This saves time when text is being formatted and helps to keep its appearance consistent throughout a publication.

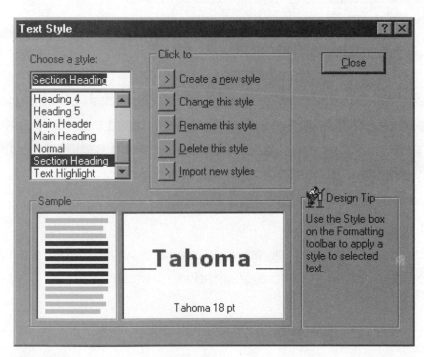

Fig 13.6: Defining a text style.

- ## Borders

   Borders can be used to make objects stand out — this may just be a coloured line or something more sophisticated as shown in Figure 13.7.

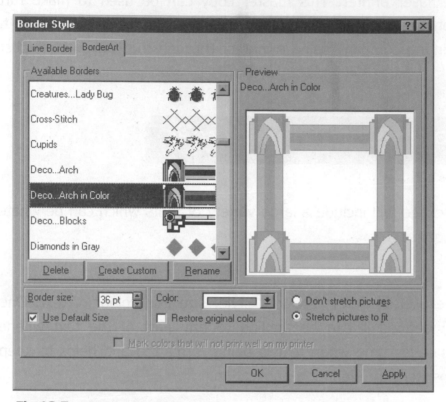

Fig 13.7: Adding a border.

- # Colour

   A good DTP package will include a large choice of colours which can be used to fill in areas of a page or make text, borders and lines stand out more. Various tints, shades and patterns of colour are usually offered along with the facility for creating a customised colour scheme for a publication.

- # Clipart

   DTP packages often have a library of artwork supplied with them from which graphics can be copied and pasted into a publication.

• Character spacing

The spacing between characters can be adjusted by using a feature called **kerning**. All DTP packages offer this facility along with options to shrink and stretch text — this is shown in Figure 13.8

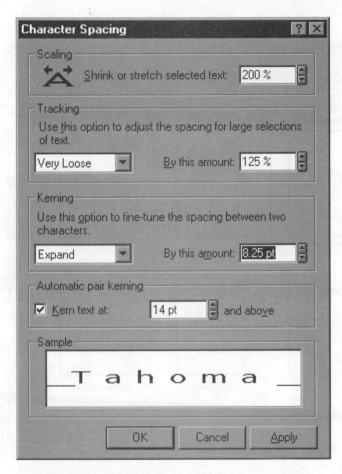

Fig 13.8: Changing character spacing

• Line spacing

The spacing between lines can be changed by adjusting the **leading** — this was explained in Chapter 12.

• Design wizards

'Design Wizards' are provided to give step-by-step help when creating common types of publication such as newspapers, newsletters, flyers and greetings cards. The design wizards offered by a typical DTP package are shown in Figure 13.9 below.

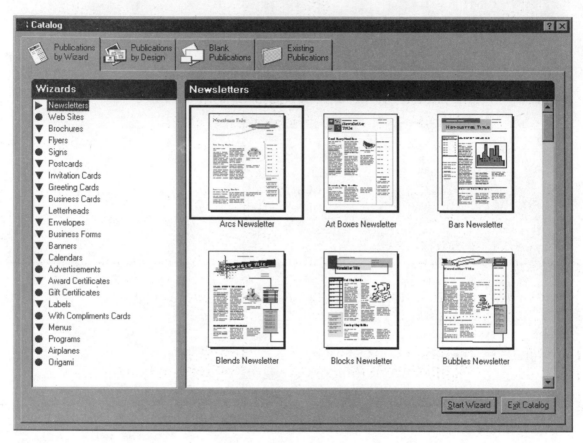

Fig 13.9: Design wizards help to save time designing page layouts.

• Text columns

DTP packages all offer a facility which allows the user to set up the pages of a publication to have a certain number of text columns. This is useful when producing a newsletter or newspaper.

Questions

1. A desktop publishing package will be used to produce an "Anti-Smoking" leaflet aimed at teenagers.

   Name **four** factors that you would have to take into account when creating this leaflet. For each, give a feature of the desktop publishing package you would use to put this factor into practice.

   For example:

   Factor — There should be no spelling mistakes in the leaflet.

   Feature of package — The spell checker can be used. (8)

   NEAB 1996 Paper 1 Tier P

2. A group of young people at a local tennis club are going to use a DTP (Desk Top Publishing) package to produce a notice to advertise a tennis summer school. Their first attempt is shown here.

   Tennis Summer School
   Dates – August 4th to August 7th
   Time – 10am to 3pm
   Chief Coach – Mrs Perry
   Clothing – suitable tennis clothing must be worn
   Cost - £20 to members, £30 to non-members
   This course is open to all age groups – come along and have fun.

   They were not very pleased with their first attempt and they have used the DTP (Desk Top Publishing) package to make a number of changes. Their new poster is shown below.

   ## Tennis Summer School

   Dates – August 4th to August 7th

   Time – 10am to 3pm

   Chief Coach – Mrs Perry

   Clothing – suitable tennis clothing must be worn

   Cost - £20 to members, £30 to non-members

   This course is open to all age groups – come along and have fun.

(a) Give **four** features of the DTP (Desk Top Publishing) package that have been used to produce the changes to the new poster. (4)

(b) Describe **three** different features of the DTP (Desk Top Publishing) package that could be used to improve the poster. Give a reason why each feature might be used. (6)

NEAB 2000 Paper 1 Tier F

3. As part of your work at school you have been asked to produce a story book for children at your local infant school.

(a) (i) Give **three** ways in which using a desktop publishing package could improve the quality of presentation of the story book as opposed to using a manual typewriter. (3)

(ii) Give two benefits, other than improving appearance, of using IT to produce this story book rather than a manual typewriter. (2)

(b) Name and give a reason for **four** factors that you would have to take into account when designing and producing a story book for children aged between 5 and 7. (6)

NEAB 1995 Paper 1 Tier R

4. For the last 10 years a history teacher has used a typewriter to produce most of her worksheets. She is about to produce a new set of worksheets for year 7 on the Romans.

(a) Explain to her the advantages of using a desktop publishing (DTP) package for this task rather than her typewriter. (8)

(b) What arguments do you think the teacher could use for continuing to use her typewriter to produce the worksheet? (3)

NEAB 1999 Paper 1 Tier H

Websites

- Visit **www.dtp.com/** for desk top publishing resources and information.
- If you use Microsoft Publisher resources and information can be found at **www.microsoft.com/office/publisher**

Chapter 14

A graphics package is an application that can be used to create and manipulate images on a computer. The images that are produced using graphics packages can be used in many different ways — some of these are listed below.

- As a source of original artwork when using word processing, DTP or presentation software;
- To produce plans and designs;
- To provide characters and backgrounds for computer games;
- To create graphics for use on a web site;
- To provide special effects for feature films and TV programmes.

Painting and drawing packages

A **painting package** produces images by changing the colour of **pixels** on the screen, which are then coded as a pattern of bits to create a **bitmapped** graphics file. Bitmapped graphics are used for images such as scanned photographs or pictures taken with a digital camera. The main advantage offered by this type of graphic is that individual pixels can be changed which makes very detailed editing possible. The disadvantages of bitmaps are:

- Individual parts of an image cannot be resized; only the whole picture can be increased or decreased in size. This can create empty spaces, jagged edges or produce a blurred image;
- Information has to be stored about every pixel in an image; this produces large files that use large amounts of backing storage space.

Examples of graphics packages that produce bitmapped images include MS Paint, PC Paintbrush, Adobe PhotoShop and JASC's Paint Shop Pro.

A **drawing package** produces images that are made up from coloured lines and shapes such as circles, squares and rectangles. When an image is saved it is stored in a **vector graphics file** as a series of instructions, which can be used to recreate it. The main advantages offered by this type of graphic are:

- They use up much less storage space than bitmap graphics;

- Each part of an image is treated as a separate object, which means that individual parts can be easily modified.

The disadvantage of vector graphics is that they don't look as realistic as bitmap graphics which makes them unsuitable for storing images like photographs. Examples of drawing graphics packages include CorelDraw, Micrographix Designer and CAD (computer aided design) packages such as AutoCAD (CAD packages are explained in more detail later in this chapter).

Common features of graphics packages

The many different graphics packages available today all have many common features. Some of these are described below.

- Drawing **straight lines** and 'freehand' lines;

- Drawing regular **pre-defined shapes** like squares, rectangles and circles using a special 'tool';

- Entering text and changing the style and size of font;

- Changing the size of an object, or **scaling** (Figure 14.1);

original object

object scaled by 200%

Fig 14.1: Scaling a graphic.

- **Rotating** objects. Objects can be rotated in a circle either clockwise or anticlockwise by specifying the direction and angle of rotation (Figure 14.2)

object before rotation   object after a 150° clockwise rotation

Fig 14.2: Rotating a graphic.

- **Stretching**. Objects can be stretched either horizontally or vertically (or even both) changing both their size and appearance (Figure 14.3);

before stretching   after **vertical** stretching   after **horizontal** stretching

Fig 14.3: Stretching a graphic.

- '**Flipping**' an object, this can be either **horizontally** or **vertically** (Figure 14.4);

ordinary object   **vertical** 'flip'   **horizontal** 'flip'

Fig 14.4: Flipping a graphic.

- A **paint palette** (Figure 14.5) from which different colours and patterns can be chosen.

Fig 14.5: A paint palette.

- A **fill** option for colouring in a shape or area on the screen with a colour or pattern from the paint palette.

un-filled object   filled object

Fig 14.6: Filling an object with colour.

- **Clipart**. Some packages have a built-in library of pictures drawn by professional artists. Most application packages are supplied with clipart.

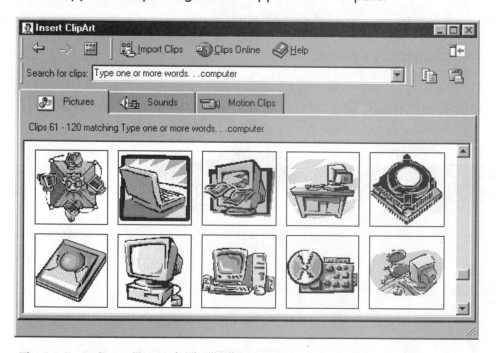

Fig 14.7: A clipart library.

- **Zoom** or **magnify** is a feature that allows an area of the screen to be seen close up for detailed work.

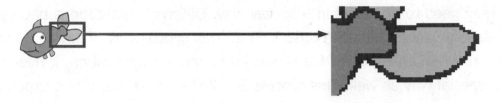

Fig 14.8: Zooming in on part of an image allows the user to see fine detail.

- **Brushes**. Special brushes such as an airbrush can be used to achieve different paint effects on the screen.

In most graphics packages features like the ones described above are chosen from a **toolbar** or **tool palette** where they are displayed as icons. Figure 14.9 below shows the toolbar of a simple graphics package.

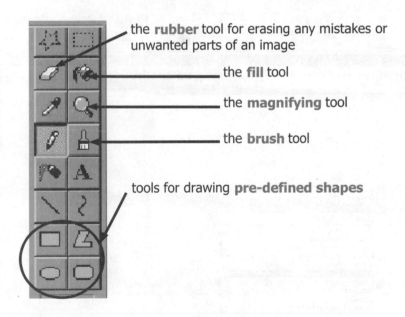

Fig 14.9: The toolbar of a graphics package.

Importing and exporting graphics files

If a picture produced using a graphics package is going to be used in another application, it may need to be saved in a special way. Different applications packages might not necessarily understand each other's **files**. This special way of saving a file is called **exporting**. When an exported file is needed in another application, it needs to be opened in a special way as well. This process is called **importing**. When exporting and importing files it is necessary to specify a **file format**. There are many different graphics file formats but most of them can be divided into two main groups. These are **vector format** and **bitmap format** files.

Vector format files use lines and angles to store information about the objects which make up the graphic image. These file type formats include:

- **CGM**   **Computer Graphics Metafile**
- **WMF**   **Windows Metafile**
- **EPS**   **Encapsulated Postscript**

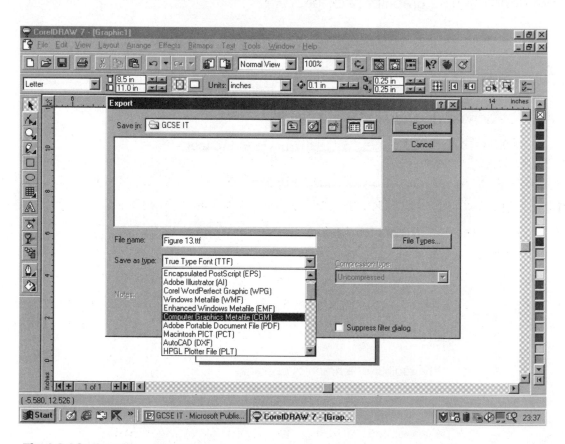

Fig 14.10: Exporting a graphic.

Bitmap format files use patterns of binary numbers to store data about the individual pixels which make up the graphic image. The format of a file determines exactly how the application will save it and, in the case of importing, what **graphics filter** to use to load a file in. The graphics filter 'translates' an exported file into a format that the application which is importing it can understand. These file type formats include:

- **TIF**   **Tagged Image File**
- **GIF**   **Graphics Interchange File**
- **JPG**   **Joint Photographic Expert Group**

Computer-aided design and manufacture

Computer-aided design, or **CAD**, is the use of a computer to display designs, accept any changes to them and calculate and display the results. CAD has many different applications but some of the more common ones are listed below.

- Designing new cars;
- Bridge and building design and testing;
- Printed circuit board (PCB) design;
- Designing new aircraft;
- Designing fitted kitchens.

Making changes to a design requires a large number of complex calculations. These need to be performed as quickly as possible so that their effect can be viewed straight away. A powerful processor is required for this. A CAD system also needs a high-resolution monitor so that the designer can see very clear close-up detail on the screen. Input to CAD systems is normally given using a mouse and keyboard but other input devices such as graphic tablets and scanners are also used. Output from a CAD system is produced using a high quality printer such as a laser printer or a plotter.

The advantages of using a CAD system rather than producing designs by hand are:-

- Changes to a design can be made quickly and their effects seen straight away;

- Designs can be viewed from any angle without being re-drawn;

- Designs can be tested without the need to build expensive models or prototypes;

- Drawings of 'standard' parts can be stored on disk and used whenever they are needed. This means that new designs which will use existing parts do not have to be drawn completely from scratch;

- Designs can be instantly sent anywhere in the world using electronic communications;

- Designs can be used directly in computer aided manufacturing processes.

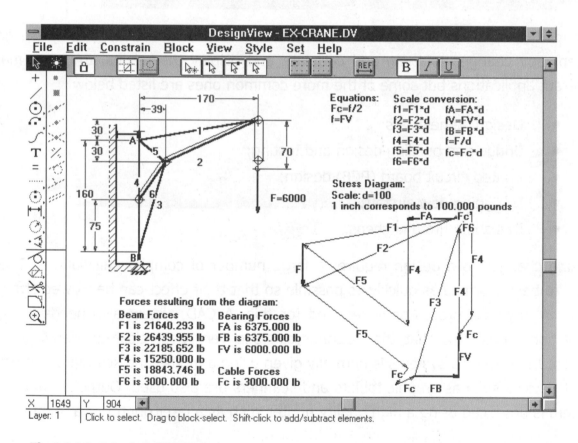

Fig 14.11: A typical CAD package.

Computer-aided manufacture, or **CAM**, is the use of a computer to control all or part of a manufacturing process. Some examples of CAM include the production of printed circuit boards, car manufacture, pattern cutting for clothing manufacture and making postage stamps. Very often a CAM process follows directly on from a CAD process, in such cases the complete design and manufacture process is called **CAD/ CAM**. The main advantage of this approach is that the CAD design can be used to generate the program which will control the manufacturing process. Figure 14.12 shows a computer-controlled milling machine being used to manufacture a design that has been prepared using a CAD package.

Fig 14.12: Manufacturing a design prepared using a CAD package.
The student shown in the picture has used CAD software to prepare a design which he is going to manufacture using the milling machine connected to the computer behind him.

The advantages of using a CAM system to manufacture goods are:-

- Products can be made very accurately and consistently;

- Around the clock production is much cheaper;

- A product's design can be modified without the need to bring production to a complete standstill;

- Waste can be kept to a minimum.

Questions

1. A school has recently bought a new graphics package. The package has **tools** that carry out various tasks. Five of the different **tools** that are available in the graphics package are given below. Explain carefully the purpose of each.

   (a) Freehand drawing (1)
   (b) Pre-defined shapes (1)
   (c) Text (1)
   (d) Copy (1)
   (e) Palette (1)

   NEAB 1998 Paper 1 Tier F

2. A company which designs and fits bedrooms is planning to buy a graphics package to produce designs that can be printed and given to its customers. Outline **five features** (other than saving and printing) that you would expect to have. (5)

   NEAB 1999 Paper 1 Tier F

3. A firm builds kitchens to order. They supply and fit all the cupboards and appliances. They could design the kitchens using a software package or they could draw all the designs by hand. Give **four** reasons why they might choose to use the software package.

   NEAB 1996 Paper 1 Tier Q

4. (a) Explain what is meant by the term Computer Aided Manufacturing (CAM). (2)
   (b) Give **three** advantages to a business of introducing a Computer Aided Manufacturing process. (3)
   (c) Give **two** possible disadvantages to a business of introducing a Computer Aided Manufacturing process. (2)

5.   (a) Explain the difference between **bitmap** and **vector** graphics.   (2)

      (b) Give **two** disadvantages of bitmapped graphics.   (2)

      (c) Give **one** example of a bitmap format file type.   (1)

      (d) Give **two** advantages of a vector graphic.   (2)

      (e) Give **one** example of a vector format file type.   (1)

      (f) Explain why a graphics filter may be needed when importing a graphics file into an application.   (2)

Websites

- For an introduction to graphics software, tips and related links visit **http://graphicssoft.about.com/compute/graphicssoft/mbody.htm**

- Visit **www.caligari.com** to find out about 3-D graphics software.

- View some samples of images produced using 3-D graphics software at **www.povray.org/java-index.html**

- Take a look at the graphics that a supercomputer can generate by visiting **www.ncsa.uiuc.edu/sdg/digitalgallery/dg_science_theater.html**

Chapter 15 Models and Simulations

Computer models are used to predict and investigate how a device or process might behave given a certain set of conditions. Computer models exist only inside the computer as a program that contains a set of rules expressed as mathematical equations — they do not take up space in the outside world. The rules of a model describe an object or process and the variables that can be changed to affect the way that it behaves. It is this set of rules that determine how good a model is — incomplete or poorly expressed rules will make inaccurate and unreliable predictions.

Some of the more common uses for computer models are: -

- Car manufacturers use models to test the effects of crashes on new cars, which is a lot more cost effective than building and crashing real cars;

- Civil engineers use models to predict the effects of natural hazards such as strong winds or earthquakes on designs for new buildings and bridges;

- Aeroplane manufacturers use models to test the aerodynamics of new designs and avoid the expense of building real planes;

- The UK Treasury uses a complicated financial model to investigate the possible effects of changes to public spending, interest rates or taxes on the economy;

- Many businesses use financial models to investigate ways of cutting down costs and improving their profitability;

- Weather forecasting services use very complicated models of the atmosphere to predict how the weather will behave;

- Scientists use computer models to investigate the effects of changes to the climate brought about by global warming.

Computer models can be built in a number of different ways. Spreadsheet packages are often used to construct simple models. For more complicated systems special programming languages designed for modelling can be used — SIMSCRIPT and SIMULA are examples of such languages. Another alternative is to use an application package specially designed for modelling. 'Model Builder' is an example of such a package. It is often used in schools to teach students how to use and build computer models.

Simulations

A computer simulation is a special type of computer model which recreates a system, that might exist outside the computer. Simulations are often used to train people how to deal with situations that are too difficult, expensive or dangerous to recreate and practise for real. The best example of a simulation is a flight simulator, which is used to train pilots (these are explained in more detail over the page). Many computer games are simulations of situations such as driving a racing car, flying a jet fighter, playing in a premiership football match, or even taking part in a futuristic battle (Figure 15.2).

Fig 15.2: A battle simulation game.

Flight simulators

Flight simulators are used to train pilots how to deal with situations that would be expensive and dangerous to practise using a real aircraft. A flight simulator consists of a working replica of the flight deck of an aeroplane, which is mounted on hydraulic supports that are used to create a realistic feeling of movement. Simulation software provides a view of the simulated outside world through the cockpit window, controls the instrument readings and responds to commands given by the pilot. The main advantage of using a flight simulator is that pilots can practise how to deal with dangerous situations without putting lives at risk or damaging expensive equipment.

Some of the advantages of using computer models and simulations are: -

- Expensive prototypes or full size mock-ups don't need to be built;
- No equipment is damaged;
- People are not put in any danger;
- Modifications can be made easily and re-tested quickly.

Some of the disadvantages of using computer models and simulations are: -

- The results depend on how good the model is — a poor model will give unreliable results;
- Simulations can't completely re-create the pressures that a person might be under in a real-life situation.

Fig 15.3: This flight simulator in the Netherlands has an actual cockpit inside the dome. Simulated scenes are projected onto the dome, and the hydraulics underneath move the unit. (Photo courtesy of Evans & Sutherland Computer Corporation.)

Questions

1. Motor manufacturers are now fitting air bags as safety features on many new cars. They use computer simulations to test how these air bags work in different crash conditions.

   (a) Give **two** reasons why computer simulations are used in this situation. (2)

   (b) After these simulations have been carried out, the air bags are tested in crash situations using real cars. Why is this necessary? (1)

   NEAB 1996 Paper 1 Tier R

2. Simulators can be used to gain experience of driving cars at high speeds.

   (a) Give **one** example of people who may need to use such a simulator as part of their job. (1)

   (b) Give **two** reasons why a simulator would be used in this situation. (2)

   (c) All simulators rely on rules built into the controlling software.
   Tick **three** boxes to show the rules that could reasonably be built into this driving simulator. (3)

	Tick **three** boxes only
Motorway driving must be fast	
Cars take longer to stop on wet roads than on dry roads	
Cars over three years old must have a valid MOT certificate	
Cars should stop at red traffic lights	
Younger drivers pay more for car insurance	

   (d) Name and briefly describe **two** other situations in which computer simulation might reasonably be used. (4)

   NEAB 1999 Paper 1 Tier F

3.   Computer models are used in a wide variety of situations, such as training pilots and simulating a leak in a nuclear reactor.

(a)   What is a computer model?   (2)

(b)   Give **three** reasons for using computer models.   (6)

NEAB 1997 Paper 1 Tier H

Websites

- Read and produce a summary of the article "THE WORLD IN A MACHINE" by Professor Paul Edwards of the University of Michigan School of Information at:
  www.si.umich.edu/~pne/modeling.world.htm#Heading2
  which describes some of the early uses of computer models and simulations.

- Read about how computer models of entire virtual cities can be constructed and used at **http://fos.bath.ac.uk/vas/papers/ARQ96/**

- The UCLA Department of Architecture and Urban Design (AUD) is building a real-time simulation model of the city of Los Angeles. Check this out at:
  www.gsaup.ucla.edu/bill/LA.html

- Find out how the Goddard Space Flight Center (GSFC) use atmospheric computer modelling at **http://hyperion.gsfc.nasa.gov/Modelling/Modelling.html**

Chapter 16 — The System Life Cycle

The **system life cycle** is a series of stages that are worked through during the development of a new information system. A lot of time and money can be wasted if a system is developed that doesn't work properly or do exactly what is required of it. A new system is much more likely to be successful if it is carefully planned and developed to meet needs that have been thoroughly investigated and identified. This is what the stages of the system life cycle (shown below in Figure 16.1) aim to do.

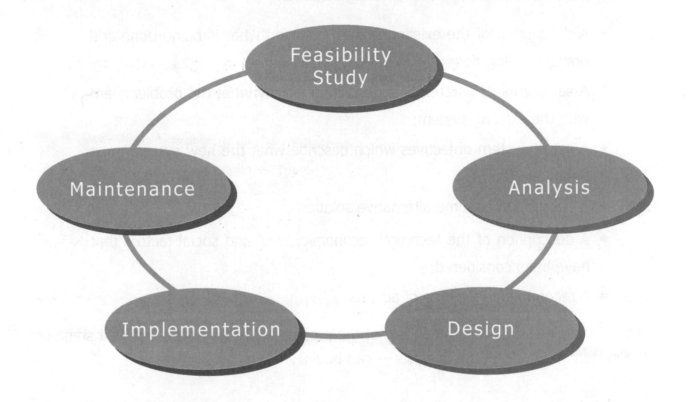

Fig 16.1: The stages of the system life cycle

It is normal for a group of people to work on the development of a new information system rather than just one person. This group is called the **system development project team**. Most of the members of this team will be **systems analysts**. A systems analyst is responsible for finding out about the existing system, designing a new system to replace it and supervising its development. The other members of the team are **programmers**. A programmer writes computer programs that match the design specifications given to them by a systems analyst.

Feasibility study

The first stage of the system life cycle is the **feasibility study**. This is an investigation that is carried out by a systems analyst to find out what the main problems are with the existing system and if it is technically possible and cost-effective to solve these problems by developing a computer based solution. The results of this investigation are presented by the systems analyst in a **feasibility report**. This report will have the following contents:-

- A description of the existing system outlining what is being done and how it is being done;

- A set of problem statements describing exactly what the problems are with the existing system;

- A set of system objectives which describe what the new system must be able to do;

- A description of some alternative solutions;

- A description of the technical, economic, legal and social factors that have been considered;

- A recommended course of action.

If the feasibility study recommends that the project should go ahead the next stage of the system life cycle — the analysis — can begin.

Analysis

During the analysis stage systems analysts investigate the existing system to answer questions such as "what is being done now?", "why is it being done?", "who is doing it?" and "how is it being done?". This information is used to identify exactly what the problems are with the existing system. During their investigation the systems analysts will use a variety of **fact-finding methods** to gather information — some of these methods are described opposite.

- **Questionnaires**

  Questionnaires are a useful way of gathering a lot of information quickly. People are often more honest and say what they really think about a system if they are filling in an anonymous questionnaire rather than being asked face-to-face in an interview. It is also much easier to analyse the responses given on a well-designed questionnaire than notes taken during interviews.

- **Interviews**

  Information can be gathered by talking to people who use the existing system and asking them what they think about it. Much more detailed information can be gathered through interviews but they can be time consuming if a lot of people need interviewing.

- **Observation**

  Watching people use a system can often give a more accurate picture of what actually happens than interviews or questionnaires. The problems with this method are that people can find it threatening to be watched while they are working and quite a lot of time is consumed as little useful information is gathered during short observations.

- **Examining documents**

  This method involves looking at the paperwork that is used in the existing system. Paperwork includes any forms that are completed, letters, memos and manual filing systems such as paper records in a filing cabinet. For systems that are already computerised screen layouts and printed output will also be examined.

Once the systems analysts have completed their investigation they produce a detailed description of how the existing system works. This will contain information about the data that is stored, where it is stored, how it flows around the system and how it is processed. Various methods are used by a systems analyst to help describe the various parts of a system. These include: **data flow diagrams** (DFDs) and **systems flowcharts**.

- **Data flow diagrams (DFDs)**

  A data flow diagram describes how data flows through a system. Data flow diagrams are concerned only with the data in a system and do not describe any of its hardware. The symbols used in data flow diagrams are described in Figure 16.2 below.

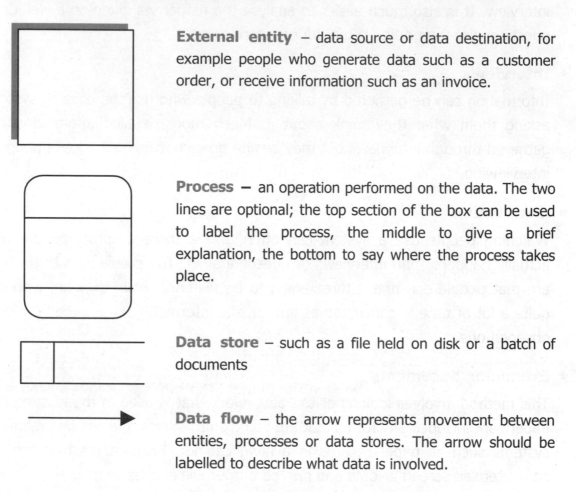

External entity – data source or data destination, for example people who generate data such as a customer order, or receive information such as an invoice.

Process – an operation performed on the data. The two lines are optional; the top section of the box can be used to label the process, the middle to give a brief explanation, the bottom to say where the process takes place.

Data store – such as a file held on disk or a batch of documents

Data flow – the arrow represents movement between entities, processes or data stores. The arrow should be labelled to describe what data is involved.

Fig 16.2: Symbols used in a data flow diagram (DFD)

Figure 16.3 opposite shows an example of a data flow diagram for a theatre booking system. The theatre uses a computerised system to store records about customers, plays and bookings. Customers can make a booking by telephoning, visiting the booking office or completing a pre-printed form and posting it to the theatre. The booking clerk checks if there are any seats available for the performance. If there are, the clerk reserves the seats, then checks whether the customer's details are already on file and, if not, types them in. The tickets are then printed out and handed or sent to the customer. Payment is made either in cash or by credit card.

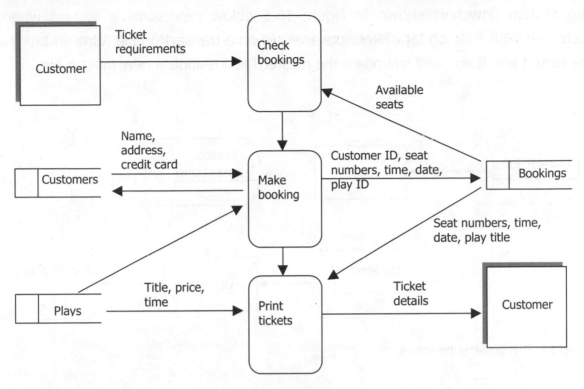

Fig 16.3: Data flow diagram for a theatre booking system.

- ### Systems flowcharts
  Systems flowcharts describe the parts of a system in terms of the hardware, the data that is stored, the processes that are carried out using this data and the resulting output. The symbols used in systems flowcharts are shown in Figure 16.4 below.

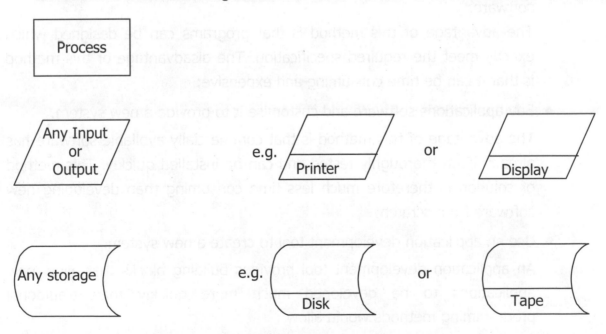

Fig 16.4: Symbols used in systems flowcharts.

The system flowchart shown in Figure 16.5 below represents a system where a customer file is held on tape. Receipts are held on a transaction file (also on tape) and are sorted and then used to update the master file, creating a new master file.

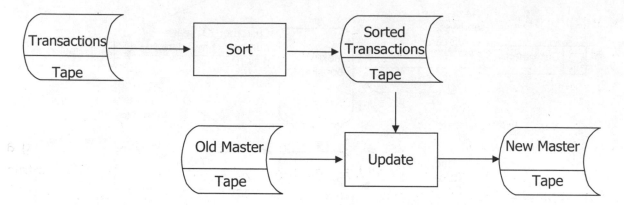

Fig 16.5: A systems flowchart.

Design

During the design stage of the system life cycle alternative possible solutions are identified. For example the following alternative methods might be considered:-

- Create the new system by using programming languages to write special software.

  The advantage of this method is that programs can be designed which exactly meet the required specification. The disadvantage of this method is that it can be time consuming and expensive;

- Buy applications software and customise it to provide a new system.

  The advantage of this method is that commercially available software has already been thoroughly tested and can be installed quickly. This method of solution is therefore much less time consuming than developing new software from scratch;

- Use an application development tool to create a new system.

  An application development tool provides building blocks that allow new applications to be developed much more quickly than traditional programming methods would allow.

Once the alternative solutions have been identified they are evaluated using the following evaluation criteria:-

- What hardware does this solution require?

- What benefits does this solution offer?

- What are the drawbacks of this solution?

- How long will it take to develop this solution?

- How much will this solution cost?

This process allows the best solution to identified so that the detailed design of the new system can begin. The rest of the design stage is concerned with producing a **design specification** that describes the new system in detail. This will contain information about the following:-

- **Input**
  - What data will need to be input?
  - What are the sources of the input data?
  - What input methods will be used?
  - What will any input screens need to look like and have on them?

- **Output**
  - What output is required from the system?
  - What output methods will be used?
  - What layout is needed on printed output?
  - What will output screens need to look like and have on them?

- **Data storage**
  - What data files are needed?
  - What fields will the records in each file need?
  - What validation checks will be used to make sure data is sensible and correct?

- **User interface**
  - Which type of user interface will be used (menu driven, graphical or command driven)?
  - What options will be available to users?

- **Backup and recovery procedures**

  – What methods will be used to back up the system?
  – How often will backups be carried out?
  – Where will backup copies be kept?
  – How will data be restored if it is lost or damaged?

- **Security procedures**

  – How will data be protected from unauthorised access?
  – Will some users need different levels of access from other users?

- **Test plan**

  A plan of the testing that will be carried out on the new system is prepared. This should include details of the purpose of each test, the test data that will be used and what the expected result is. A test plan should also include space where reference can be made to the actual result of the test and where the evidence of this can be found. Figure 16.6 below shows a typical format for a test plan.

Test N°	Test Data	Purpose	Expected Result	Actual Result
1	Enter incorrect mark '–1'	Test input mark function	Mark rejected	
2	Enter incorrect mark '45'	Test input mark function	Mark accepted	
3	Enter new student with student_number '100' forename 'David' surname 'Cooke'	Test 'Add new student' function	'David Cooke' added to the student database	

Fig 16.6: A typical test plan format.

Implementation

The stage of the system life cycle involves:-

- Setting up the system so that it matches the design specification. As we have already discussed this may involve writing new programs, customising existing commercial software or using application development tools. Whatever the method used some of the activities at this stage will include the following:-

  - Creating data files;
  - Setting up data validation checks;
  - Entering enough data ready for testing the system;
  - Creating input and output screens;
  - Setting up the user interface;
  - Setting up system security.

- Testing is carried out using the plan prepared during the design stage to make sure that all the parts of the system work correctly with **normal**, **extreme** and **erroneous** data. These three types of test data are described below.

  - Normal test data is used to check that a system can handle the sort of data that would be expected during day-to-day use;

  - Extreme test data is used to check that a system can cope with data that lies on the boundaries of what is acceptable;

  - Erroneous (or exceptional) test data is used to check that a system can identify data that is wrong and reject it;

Figure 16.7 over the page shows a test plan with these three types of test data in it. The tests listed are being used to check part of a system which is used to input student examination marks in the range 0 to 100.

Test 1 uses **normal** test data to check that the system will accept marks within the allowed range.

Tests 2 and 3 use **extreme** test data to check that the system will accept marks on the boundaries of the allowed range — in this case 0 and 100.

Test 4 uses **erroneous** test data to check that the system will reject marks outside the allowed range.

Test N°	Test Data	Purpose	Expected Result	Actual Result
1	Enter a mark of '50' ; this is within the range	Test input mark function	Mark accepted	
2	Enter a mark of '0' ; this is on the limit of the range	Test input mark function	Mark accepted	
3	Enter a mark of '100' ; this is on the limit of the range	Test input mark function	Mark accepted	
4	Enter a mark of '101' ; this is out of the range	Test input mark function	Mark rejected	

Fig 16.7: Testing using **normal**, **extreme** and **erroneous** data.

- Installing the new system; this might include any of the following activities:-

  - Installing any new hardware and software;
  - Transferring data from the existing system to the new one;
  - Training users how to operate the new system.

  There are many different ways that a new information system can be introduced — some of the more common ones are described below.

  Direct implementation involves changing from using the old system one day to using the new one the next. This is the quickest way of introducing a new system but can be very disruptive if any errors are found afterwards.

  Parallel implementation (or parallel running) involves operating the new system and the old system alongside each other for a short period of time. This has the advantage that problems with the new system can be sorted out without any disruption. The disadvantage of this method is that it can be difficult and stressful for staff to try and operate two systems at once.

  Phased implementation involves introducing the new system in smaller parts while leaving the remaining parts of the old system in place.

- Producing **documentation** for the system: there are two types of documentation — **technical documentation** and **user documentation**.

Technical documentation describes a system in detail in terms that a systems analyst or programmer can understand if changes need to be made to it. This will include things like:

- the system design specification;
- systems flowcharts;
- data flow diagrams;
- a description of the various parts of the system and what each one does;
- screen layouts and user interface designs;
- the test plan.

User documentation provides the people who will be using a system with information about what it can do, how to operate it and how to deal with error messages. Good user documentation should contain the following sections:

- a description of what the system is designed to do;
- minimum hardware and software requirements of the system;
- instructions on how to load and run the system;
- detailed instructions on how to operate each part of the system;
- Error messages, their meaning and how to deal with them.
- Where to get more help, such as telephone support lines and on-line tutorials.

- Carrying out a **post-implementation review** after the new system has been running for a few weeks or months to identify any modifications that may need to be made.

Maintenance

After a new information system has been successfully installed and running for some time it may need to be changed. This could be due to a change in the needs of the user, to correct problems not found during testing, or simply to improve the way the system works.

Questions

1. A Video Games shop has decided to use a spreadsheet to help with its finances. The tasks listed below have to be carried out during the development of this system.

    A   Entering all the existing data for the income and expenditure of the shop
    B   Working out the spreadsheet structure
    C   Looking at the present system to see how it works
    D   Finding out if the new system works
    E   Setting up the spreadsheet
    F   Reviewing how well the new system works
    G   Making a test plan

    Using the letters A to G from the list of tasks, answer the following questions.

    Which one of these takes place during the analysis stage?
    Which two of these take place during the design stage?
    Which one of these takes place during the testing stage?
    Which two of these take place during the implementation stage?
    Which one of these takes place during the evaluation stage?   (7)

    NEAB 1998 Paper 1 Tier F

2. When a new computerised system is being developed it is important that it is properly tested and documented.

    (a) A package processes examination marks. When the marks are input they have to be validated with a range check. Marks are allowed if they are in the range 0 to 100.
    Give **three** numbers you would use to test the range check worked correctly.
    Explain why you would carry out each of your three tests.   (6)

    (b) Documentation supplied with a system should provide instructions for normal use. Describe **three** other topics which should be included in the User Guide.   (3)

    NEAB 1998 Paper 2 Tier F

4. Draw and label a diagram to show the main stages of the system life cycle. (6)

5. When a new computerised system is suggested, a full analysis of user requirements has to be carried out. Describe the methods which can be used to find out about an existing system and what will be needed in the new system. Discuss the advantages and disadvantages of the methods used.

(12)

NEAB 1998 Paper 2 Tier H

6. The partners of a doctors' surgery are considering using a computer system to store patient records and handle appointments. A systems analyst is called in to carry out a feasibility study.

(a) Explain why a feasibility study is carried out. (3)

(b) After the feasibility study, the decision is made to go ahead with the introduction of the computer system. The systems analyst then carries out a detailed analysis of the existing system. Give **three** ways that the systems analyst could find out about the existing system. (3)

(c) After the analysis the systems analyst then produces a design specification for the new system. Give **four** items that should be included in the design specification. (4)

NEAB 2000 Paper 2 Tier F

Websites

- To find out more about what systems analysts do visit the Computer Museum's web site at **www.tcm.org/resources/cmp-careers/cnc-sysanalyst.html**
- For more information on data flow diagrams visit the Applied Information Science site at **www.aisintl.com/case/dfd.html**

Chapter 17

A computer network is a collection of computers that have been linked together so that they can communicate with each other allowing them to share hardware, software and data. On a typical network application software and users' data files are stored on a powerful central computer called a **file server** or just `server` for short. The server manages the resources available to network users. A computer that is not connected to a network is called a **stand-alone** computer. The PCs that people use at home are stand-alone computers.

There are two different sorts of computer network. In a `**Local Area Network**' or `**LAN**' the computers are all in the same building or in different buildings on one site. The computers in a LAN are all permanently connected to each other with special cables. Most school networks are LAN's.

In a `**Wide Area Network**' or `**WAN**' the computers are spread over a large geographical area. This might be around a town, a country or even in different continents. The computers in a WAN are not permanently connected to each other with cables, they communicate with each other using telephone lines, radio transmitters or satellite links. The Internet is an example of a WAN.

Local area network (LAN)

Each computer on a LAN is called a **workstation**. All of the workstations are connected to each other and to the server. The server is the heart of the LAN, and stores all the applications software and data needed by users as well as a list of all the network users and their passwords. Larger local area networks often have more than one server.

To use a LAN you have to identify yourself to the server by giving your **user identity** and **password**. This is called **logging on**; when you have done this you can run programs and load any files that you have saved on a previous occasion. Once you have finished using the network you **log off**, which disconnects you from the file server until you log on again. Figure 17.1 opposite shows a typical example of a local area network.

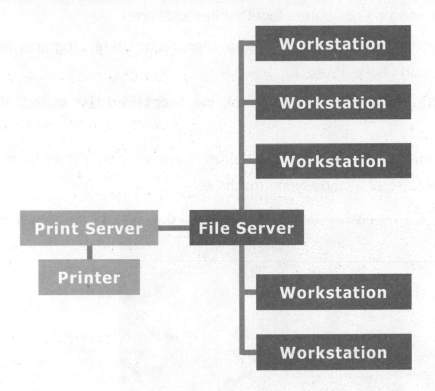

Fig 17.1: Typical components of a local area network

Some of the advantages of connecting computers together in a LAN are:-

- Workstations can share peripheral devices like printers. This is cheaper than buying a printer for every workstation;

- Workstations don't necessarily need their own hard disk or CD-ROM drives which makes them cheaper to buy than stand-alone PC's;

- Users can save their work centrally on the network's file server. This means that they can retrieve their work from any workstation on the network. They don't need to go back to the same workstation all the time;

- Users can communicate with each other and transfer data between workstations very easily;

- One copy of each application package such as a word processor, spreadsheet etc can be loaded onto the file server and shared by all users. When a new version comes out, it only has to be loaded onto the server instead of onto every workstation.

The disadvantages of connecting computers together in a LAN are:-

- Special security measures are needed to stop users from using programs and data that they shouldn't have access to;

- Networks are difficult to set up and must be maintained by skilled ICT Technicians;

- If the file server develops a serious fault all the users are affected, rather than just one user in the case of a stand-alone machine.

Fig 17.2: Students using the local area network in a school

Network security measures

There are a number of different security measures which are used on networks to protect programs and data. The main threats come from other users and hackers who might try to gain unauthorised access to programs and data and cause damage either deliberately or accidentally as a result.

- Data can be kept secure by giving each network user their own **user identity** and protecting access to it with a **password**. Individual data files can also be protected with their own password. Figure 17.3 opposite shows a network log on screen — a username and password are needed to gain access to this network.

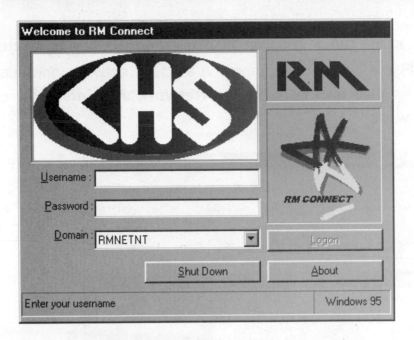

Fig 17.3: A network log on screen.

When using passwords <u>you should</u>:-

- Choose a password that is at least five characters long — if your password is too short it will be much easier for someone to watch you typing it in and remember what it is;
- Use a combination of letters and numbers in your password;
- Change your password regularly.

When using passwords <u>you should not</u>:-

- Use words that can be found in a dictionary — these can be easily found using a password cracking program or guessed if someone sees you typing part of the word;
- Use your name or nickname, date of birth, a friend's name or the name of a relative — all of these stand a good chance of being correctly guessed by anyone who knows you;
- Write your password down where it can be found easily such as underneath the keyboard.

- Unauthorised access can be reduced by allowing different users different **levels of access** (Figure 17.4) For example, on a school network individual students can only access their own work but the **Network Administrator** can access any student's work;

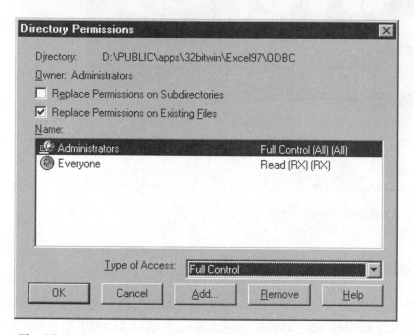

Fig 17.4: Setting levels of access to files on a network.

- Local area networks can be protected by physically **restricting access** to the computer room. This is most easily done by simply locking the door or providing users with an entry code or special 'swipe card' key.

Fig 17.5: Using a keypad lock to physically restrict access to a computer room.

Wide Area Network (WAN)

Unlike the computers in a LAN, the computers of a WAN are not permanently connected to each other with cables. The computers in a wide area network are often connected to each other using telephone lines. When a computer uses an ordinary telephone line to connect to another computer, a **modem** is needed at each end of the link. If an entire LAN needs to be connected to a WAN a special **gateway** needs to be set-up. This allows any computer on the LAN to communicate with any computer on the WAN (Figure 17.5).

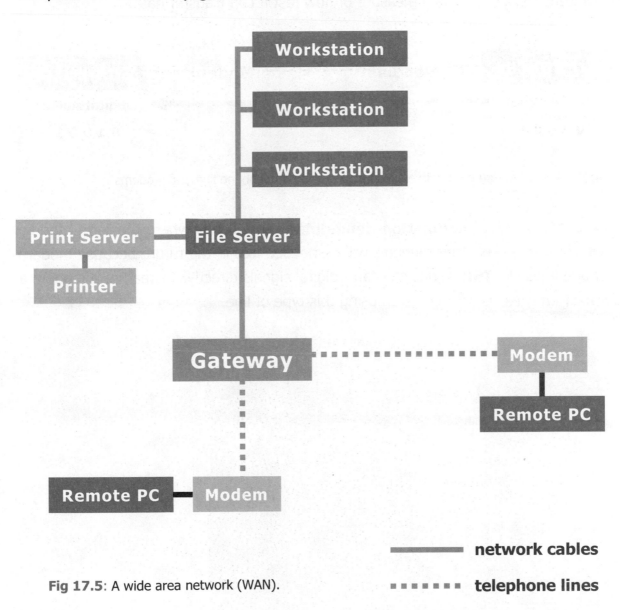

Fig 17.5: A wide area network (WAN).

──────── **network cables**

▪▪▪▪▪▪▪▪ **telephone lines**

Modems

Telephone lines are designed to carry voice signals, which are **analogue** and can have any number of different values. The **digital signals** generated by computers are made up from binary patterns of 0s and 1s and can't be transmitted along ordinary telephone lines. A **modem** converts a digital signal to an equivalent analogue signal so that it can be sent down a telephone line. At the destination another modem is needed to convert the analogue signal back into a digital signal, which the receiving computer can understand (Figure 17.6). The speed of a modem is measured in **bits per second** (bps) — this is a measure of how fast it can transfer data.

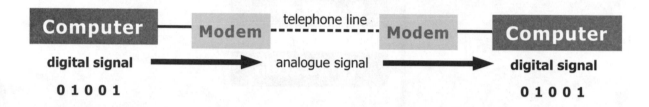

Fig 17.6: Exchanging data between computers using a telephone line and modems

This process is called **modulation-demodulation**, which is where the term modem comes from. It is likely that modems will be needed less in the future because modern telephone lines like **ISDN** lines can carry digital signals directly. Instead of a modem a **terminal adapter** is needed when using this type of line.

Questions

1. (a) What do the terms **LAN** and **WAN** stand for? (2)

    (b) Give **two** differences between a LAN and a WAN. (2)

    (c) Give **three** advantages of connecting computers together
    into a network. (3)

    (d) Give **two** disadvantages of connecting computers together
    into a network. (2)

2. Explain briefly what is meant by the following terms.

    (a) workstation (1)

    (b) file server (1)

    (c) user identity (1)

    (d) password (1)

    (e) log on (1)

3. (a) Explain why special security measures are needed on a network. (2)

    (b) Describe **two** measures that can be used to protect data on a
    network. (2)

4. A school has a local area network (LAN).

    (a) Describe the differences between a LAN and a wide area network. (2)

    (b) Give **three** advantages of having the school computers connected to a
    LAN as opposed to having the same number of stand-alone machines. (3)

    (c) Give **two** disadvantages of having the school computers connected to a
    LAN as opposed to having the same number of stand-alone machines. (2)

NEAB 1997 Paper 2 Tier H

Websites

- To find out more about networks visit
  www.iupui.edu/ithome/training/quickdocs/netintro.html
  http://ftp.yggdrasil.com/bible/TheGuide/toplevel/net/node3.html
  www.peppy.demon.co.uk/networks/index.htm

- Visit **www.howstuffworks.com/modem.htm** to find out more about how a
  modem works.

Chapter 18

One of the most important ways that information technology is used today is to distribute, exchange and share information. Electronic communication systems are what we use to do this. The most widely used forms of electronic communication are **Viewdata**, **e-mail**, **videoconferencing**, **computer networks** and the **Internet**.

Viewdata

Viewdata, or **Videotext**, looks like teletext but is different because, unlike teletext, it allows two-way communication to take place. The reason for this is that videotext is transmitted along telephone lines via a **modem**. Before the Internet, Viewdata systems were used to do things like shopping from home, or book train seats, aircraft seats, theatre tickets and holidays. Prestel, a Viewdata system operated by BT, still allows its subscribers to do these sorts of things. Perhaps the most common use of Viewdata now is by travel agents to book holidays (Figure 18.1) since many of the other things that people once used Viewdata systems like Prestel for, they can now do using the Internet.

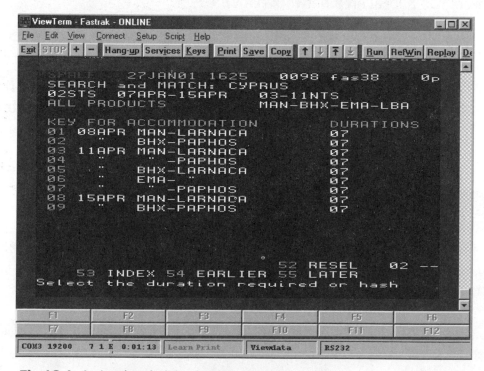

Fig 18.1: A viewdata holiday booking screen

Faxes

A fax machine scans paper documents and converts them into **digital format**. The digital version of whatever has been scanned is then converted into **analogue format** and sent over an ordinary telephone line to another fax machine. The fax machine at the receiving end converts the analogue information back into digital format and reproduces an exact hard copy of the original document.

Faxes are particularly useful for transferring images such as plans, drawings or documents with signatures between remote locations when it is important that an identical copy of the original is received at the other end. It is also possible to send and receive faxes using a personal computer if it has a fax-modem attached.

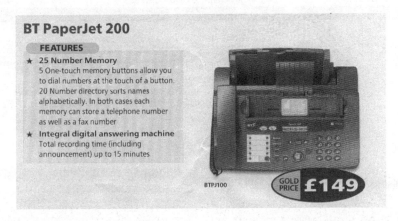

BT PaperJet 200

FEATURES
★ **25 Number Memory**
5 One-touch memory buttons allow you to dial numbers at the touch of a button. 20 Number directory sorts names alphabetically. In both cases each memory can store a telephone number as well as a fax number
★ **Integral digital answering machine**
Total recording time (including announcement) up to 15 minutes

BTPJ100

GOLD PRICE **£149**

Fig 18.2: A FAX machine.

E-mail

E-mail, or **electronic mail**, is used to send messages from one computer to another. E-mail can be sent between computers on a local area network or between computers on the Internet.

To use e-mail the user types in their message along with the **e-mail address** of the person that it is being sent to. The message is then converted into an electronic format by the computer. The 'electronic' version of the message is then sent, or **'routed'** to its destination.

If e-mail is being sent internally on a local area network it is just transferred along the network cables. E-mail being sent between computers that are a long way from each other is transferred along communications links such as telephone lines.

Incoming messages are collected and stored by the recipient's **e-mail service provider** on a central computer called a **mail server** until they open their **'electronic mailbox'** and download them. Once a message has been downloaded it can be read, saved, deleted, printed out or forwarded to another user.

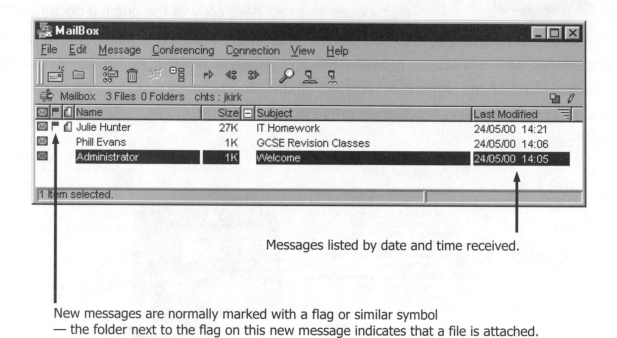

Messages listed by date and time received.

New messages are normally marked with a flag or similar symbol
— the folder next to the flag on this new message indicates that a file is attached.

Fig 18.3: An e-mail user's mailbox

Some of the advantages of using e-mail are:-

• E-mail arrives at its destination in at most a few hours, and often in a few minutes rather than in a day or two through the conventional post;

• You can send and receive e-mail anywhere in the world (and at any time) as long as you have a computer with a modem and access to a telephone line and the Internet. In fact soon you won't really need this anymore because modern mobile phones will be able to send and receive e-mail;

- One e-mail message can be sent to a group of people just as easily as it can be sent to just one person;

- Registered e-mail can be sent which will mail the sender confirmation when the mail has been read;

- E-mail can be cheaper than sending mail through the post because even long documents can be sent to the other side of the world for the price of a local telephone call;

- You can attach a file containing, say a scanned photograph which can be viewed on screen or printed out.

Some of the disadvantages of using e-mail are:-

- Some office workers and managers receive so many e-mails that they are unable to answer them all and some may simply be ignored. If they go away on holiday their mailboxes can overflow and messages may never be received;

- Computer viruses are often sent by e-mail and can damage your computer;

- People can send junk mail which you don't want just as they can with the conventional post.

Videoconferencing

The telephone or e-mail can be used by people to exchange information and ideas in real time. Using these forms of communication in this way is called **teleconferencing**. A more advanced form of teleconferencing is **videoconferencing** which is the use of a computer to send sound and video images from one computer to another in real time.

To videoconference you need:-

- A computer with a large memory and a fast processor which can handle the large amount of data that video pictures contain;

- A digital video camera to capture the video pictures at your end of the link;

- A microphone or telephone hand-set to capture the sound that goes with your pictures;

- Access to an ISDN telephone line. This is because ordinary telephone lines weren't designed to cope with the large amount of data that needs to be sent along them for videoconferencing;

- Special videoconferencing software.

Some of the advantages of videoconferencing are:-

- You can communicate with other people over long distances and see them as well as hear them. Being able to see the person at the other end of the link can be very useful if you can't rely on sound and need to use sign language for example;

- Videoconferencing is more personal than just a telephone call;

- Businesses can use videoconferencing to hold meetings which many people can be involved in;

- There is less need for people to travel which saves money and helps the environment by cutting down on pollution from cars and other non-environmentally friendly forms of transport.

Some of the disadvantages of videoconferencing are:-

- The hardware and software needed for a videoconferencing system are very expensive;
- Not many people have videoconferencing systems so the number of people that you can communicate with is very limited;
- ISDN lines are needed which are expensive to set-up and use;
- There is no substitute for a face-to-face meeting. Eye contact and body language can be as important in a business meeting as on your first date!

Teleworking

Teleworking, or **telecommuting**, is made possible by electronic communications. Telecommuting is when people work from home instead of travelling to work and use methods of electronic communication such as the telephone, fax machine, e-mail, the Internet and videoconferencing to communicate with the outside world.

Some of the advantages of telecommuting are:

- Time isn't wasted travelling to and from work;

- Cars are kept off the roads which helps the environment;

- Working at home is less stressful and it is much easier to concentrate;

- Working hours are more flexible and can be fitted around other things that need doing such as collecting children from school;

- People who live large distances away from each other can work together without having to meet in person;

- Businesses need smaller offices and spend less on light and heating.

Some of the disadvantages of telecommuting are:

- Workers may miss the company of their co-workers and feel isolated;

- Having your workplace at home might mean that you end up doing too much work and not having enough time off;

- It is more difficult for mangers to monitor and control the workforce.

Questions

1. (a) Explain what is meant by the term **e-mail**. (1)

    (b) Give **two** items of hardware that are needed to use e-mail. (2)

    (c) Do you think that e-mail will ever completely replace the ordinary post? Explain your answer carefully. (2)

2. More and more businesses are using e-mail (electronic mail) as a method of communication with their customers. Give **two** advantages with reasons for using e-mail compared with other methods of communication such as fax or telephone or post. (4)

    NEAB 2000 Paper 1 Tier H

3 . (a) Explain what is meant by the term **videoconferencing**. (2)

    (b) Explain why a videoconferencing system needs a computer with a large memory and a powerful processor. (2)

    (c) Give **four** advantages of videoconferencing. (4)

    (d) Give **one** disadvantage of videoconferencing. (1)

4. Explain what is meant by the term **teleworking** and briefly discuss some of its possible benefits and drawbacks. (5)

Websites

- Look up definitions of the key words highlighted in this chapter using the free on-line dictionary of computing at **http://wombat.doc.ic.ac.uk/foldoc/**

- Write a short article that summarises the benefits and drawbacks of teleworking using the article at **www.city.ac.uk/~db525/teleworking.html**

- To find out more about videoconferencing and how it can be used in the classroom visit **www.kn.pacbell.com/wired/vidconf/index.html**

- Visit **www.uwannawhat.com/netcourse/internet/netch3pg2.html** for tips on how to use e-mail.

Chapter 19

The Internet links private PCs, public networks and business networks together using telephone lines to form one vast world-wide network. It allows computer users to share and exchange information with each other wherever they are in the world. The information that is found on the Internet comes in many different formats. These range from simple e-mail text files to music, video clips, computer software and even live television pictures.

Connecting to the Internet

To connect to the Internet, a computer with a modem and access to a telephone line is needed. A faster connection is possible with a special type of digital telephone line called an ISDN line which doesn't need a modem. Many schools now use ISDN lines to connect the computers on their local area networks to the Internet but they are still quite expensive for home users. Some larger organisations use a **leased line** as their method of connection. A leased line is a private telephone line which is permanently open 24 hours a day. Very high speed digital lines are available but these cost hundreds of thousands of pounds per year to use. When the computers on a local area network need to be connected to the Internet using an ISDN or leased line a device called a **router** is needed. A router is a special piece of hardware which co-ordinates the switching of messages between the computers on the local area network and the rest of the Internet.

Over the next few years other methods of connecting to the Internet will become more common. The current generation of mobile phones — **WAP** (Wireless Application Protocol) — allows users to view cut down text-based versions of selected web sites or send and receive e-mail. The next generation of mobile phones, called **3G**, will allow access to any web site which will be displayed on a small touch-sensitive LCD screen. Some digital TV services now offer access to the Internet and e-mail through the television without the need for a computer.

Once you have chosen a method of connection, the next step is to find an **Internet Service Provider** (**ISP**). An Internet Service Provider is a commercial organisation, which provides a connection to the Internet for other businesses or individuals. ISPs make a small monthly charge for providing a connection. Users must also pay for the time spent using the telephone when they are 'on-line'. Charges are made for time, not distance, at local call rates.

The World Wide Web (WWW)

The **World Wide Web**, or **WWW** for short, is the largest part of the Internet. It is a body of information that spans the entire Internet. Individuals and organisations provide their own pages of information, which begin at their '**home page**'. The information pages on the World Wide Web are linked together using **hypertext**. Pages of hypertext have special keywords highlighted in a different colour from the rest of the text. By clicking on a hypertext keyword the user can go straight to other pages of information, which relate to that particular keyword. These 'related pages' might not necessarily even be on the same part of the Internet. Hypertext can be generated using **Hypertext Mark-up Language**, or **HTML**.

```
chts_tctrust - Notepad
File   Edit   Search   Help
<html>
<head>
<title>indexhome</title>
<meta http-equiv="Content-Type" content="text/html; charset=iso-
<script language="JavaScript">
<!--
function MM_swapImgRestore() { //v2.0
  if (document.MM_swapImgData != null)
    for (var i=0; i<(document.MM_swapImgData.length-1); i+=2)
      document.MM_swapImgData[i].src = document.MM_swapImgData[i
}

function MM_preloadImages() { //v2.0
  if (document.images) {
    var imgFiles = MM_preloadImages.arguments;
```

Fig 19.1: The HTML code for part of a page of hypertext

Browsers

To browse or **'surf'** the Internet for information a **browser** program is required. The most commonly used browsers are **Microsoft Internet Explorer** and **Netscape Navigator**. These browsers use **search engines**, which allow users to search for and retrieve information by entering **keywords**. There are a huge number of search engines scattered around the Internet besides those used within the most common browsers.

One of the most popular search engines is called **Yahoo!** — the Yahoo! web site is shown in Figure 19.2 below.

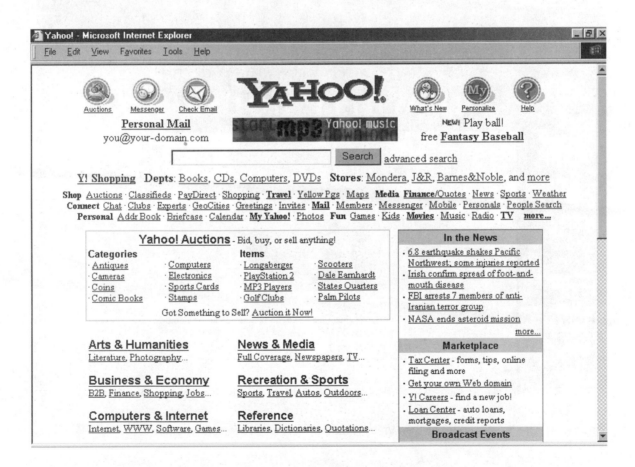

Fig 19.2: The 'home page' of Yahoo! A popular search engine

URLs

Web addresses give the location of individual sites on the World Wide Web. A web site can be quickly accessed using its address which is often referred to as a **URL** or **Uniform Resource Locator**. Most URLs start with **http//:www.** followed by a specific **site address** which is sub-divided with full-stops and 'forward slashes' (/).

For example the Web address for the 'home page' of the White House shown in Figure 19.3 below is: **http://www.whitehouse.gov**

Web site addresses often reveal the country of origin such as **.uk** for the United Kingdom. They also indicate whether the site is commercial with either **.co** or **.com**, a government organisation with **.gov**, or an academic organisation with **.ac**

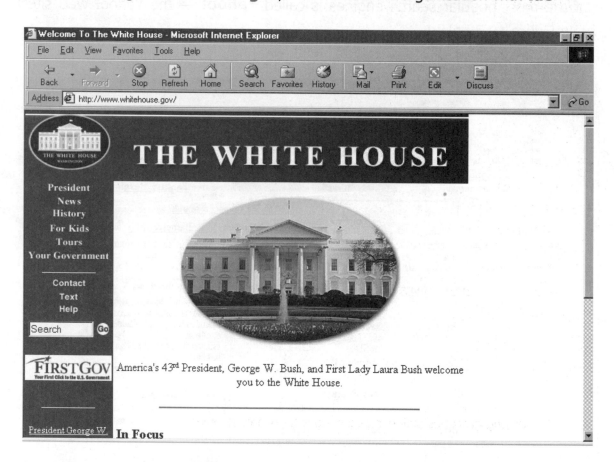

Fig 19.3: The 'home page' of the White House at **www.whitehouse.gov**

Online shopping

Many businesses now have websites that allow Internet users to buy their goods or services online at any time of day or night throughout the year. This type of online shopping also offers the advantages of not needing to travel anywhere or get pushed around in crowded shops.

One increasingly popular type of online shopping is that offered by supermarkets which allows customers to order their groceries from home and have them delivered to the door. Figure 19.4 below shows the home page of Tesco's online shopping service which was the first to be launched by a UK supermarket.

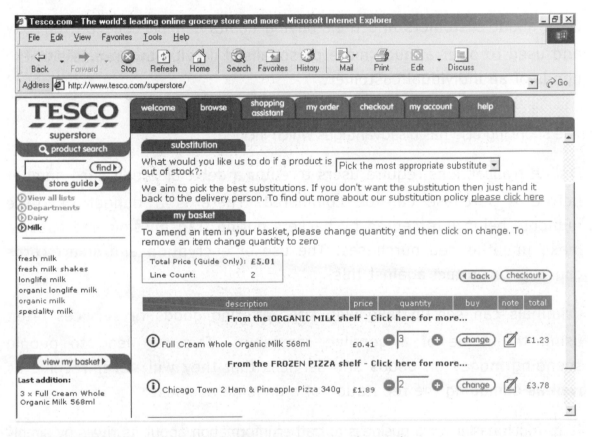

Fig 19.4: Buying groceries online is becoming increasingly popular.

Many businesses now have websites that allow Internet users to buy their goods or services online at any time of day or night throughout the year. This type of online shopping also offers the advantages of not needing to travel anywhere or get pushed around in crowded shops. There are even some companies who do all of their business over the Internet and have no ordinary shops.

There are many advantages of doing business this way, including:

- Money doesn't have to be spent on normal business overheads like renting shops and paying employees.

- Customers can be offered a much wider choice of goods because they can be ordered from suppliers as required rather than having to be kept available on the shelves all the time.

- Money is not tied up in unsold stock or wasted on products that aren't popular.

- Data about customers and their buying habits can be collected directly and used to offer a much more personalised service tailored to suit the needs of an individual customer.

Online shopping also has disadvantages which include:

- Online transactions require users to enter a debit or credit card number before a purchase can be completed. There is a danger of these numbers being intercepted by hackers during transmission and used to make unauthorised purchases. The use of encryption and smart cards can help to protect against this.

- Criminals can set up fake web sites offering goods or services often using the name of a genuine company. This can lead to people spending money on goods and services that they will never receive as well as damaging the reputation of a genuine business.

- It is much easier for a business to gather information about its rivals by simply accessing their web sites — this can make it much harder to remain competitive.

Online booking systems

Online booking systems allow Internet users to check the availability of and book things like:

- Theatre, cinema and concert tickets;
- Seats on coaches, trains and aeroplanes;
- Hotel rooms.

An online booking system is essentially a web site that can be used to access a remote database. Suppose, for example, that you wanted to reserve a hotel room. If the hotel had an online booking system available on its web site you would be able to specify the date of your arrival, length of stay and type of room required. This information would be sent over the Internet and used to search the hotel's room reservations database to see if any rooms were available that matched your request. If a room was available you would be able to reserve it by entering your personal details and credit card number – the details of your reservation would then be sent to the hotel and its reservations database would be updated instantly.

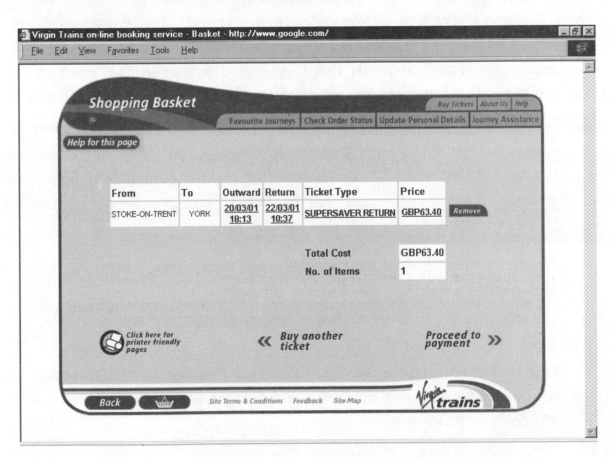

Fig 19.5: Buying a train ticket using an online booking website.

Dangers of the Internet

Connecting to the Internet is not without its dangers. Going 'on-line' exposes your computer to threats from **hackers** and **viruses**.

Hackers can gain remote access to any computer that is on the other end of an open connection to the Internet. Special **'firewall'** software can be installed on computers to try and prevent unauthorised access by providing a barrier between them and rest of the Internet.

The threat of viruses infecting your computer is perhaps more common than that posed by hackers. Whenever you read e-mail or 'download' files from the Internet you could also be letting viruses loose on your system. E-mail viruses, which infect your system the minute that you open up a message to read it, are the most common source of virus infection on computers today. In recent years the Melissa and Lovebug viruses have caused problems globally forcing businesses to shut their e-mail systems down and lose millions of pounds.

Viruses can be dealt with using a **'virus checking'** program. Many virus checking programs now come complete with an 'on-line virus check'. This checks e-mail and files for viruses as they are downloaded and alerts the user if any are detected. The problem with some e-mail viruses is that they spread so rapidly that most of the damage has already been done before virus checking software can be updated to deal with them.

There are also dangers in using the Internet at school and at home where children have access to it. There are a lot of websites that contain pornography and other undesirable material. Some of the measures that both schools and parents can take to prevent children from accessing undesirable websites are:

- Use software that blocks sites and prevents users from typing certain words into search engines when they are searching the web;
- Supervise access to the Internet by always having an adult present when it is being used;
- Use an ISP that offers a filtered service. This means that only certain 'allowed sites' can be viewed and sites known to be a problem are blocked — this is shown in Figure 19.6 opposite.

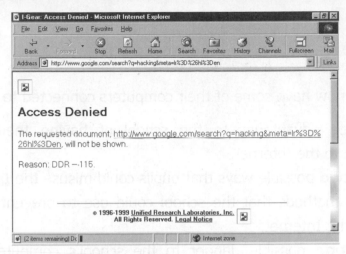

Fig 19.6: ISP filtering of undesirable web sites.

Some of the advantages of the Internet are:-

- Easy communication with other people all around the world;

- Valuable learning resource because Internet skills will be needed for jobs in the future;

- Enables more people to work from home;

- A vast amount of information can be accessed;

- Up-to-date information can be accessed on-line without the need to await publication;

- Publishing documents on the Internet saves paper;

- The Internet is a valuable resource for companies to advertise and conduct business.

Some of the disadvantages of the Internet are:-

- Much of the information isn't checked and may be incorrect or irrelevant;

- A large amount of undesirable material, such as pornography, is readily available;

- Messages sent across the Internet can be easily intercepted and are open to abuse by others;

- Large telephone bills can be easily run up;

- Too much time spent on the Internet could result in a lack of face-to-face interaction with others and a loss of social skills;

- Going on-line runs the risk of hackers or viruses being able to damage your computer.

Questions

1. Many schools now have some of their computers connected to the Internet.

   (a) Give **three** advantages to the school of having their computers connected to the Internet. (3)

   (b) Describe **two** possible ways that pupils could misuse the Internet. (2)

   (c) Give **two** methods that the school could use to prevent pupils from misusing the Internet. (2)

   (d) Describe **one** possible danger to the school's computers of being directly connected to the Internet. (1)

2. Explain briefly what is meant by the following terms.

   (a) **website** (1)

   (b) **home page** (1)

   (c) **hyperlink** (1)

   (d) **upload** (1)

   (e) **download** (1)

3. A school library has recently been extended to include an IT resources centre. This has 6 multi-media PCs which are all connected to the Internet.

   (a) Give **two possible** advantages to pupils of using CD-ROMs to find information rather than the traditional method of looking up the information in books. (2)

   (b) Give **two possible** advantages to pupils of using the Internet to find information rather than a CD-ROM. (2)

   (c) Give two **possible** reasons why some school library users will still look up information in books. (2)

   NEAB 1999 Paper 1 Tier H

4. Do you agree or disagree with the statement, "The Internet will create a world full of anti-social couch potatoes"? Explain your answer carefully. (5)

5.   Many businesses now offer online shopping services on their web sites.

   (a) What is an online shopping service? (2)

   (b) Give **two** advantages to a business of selling goods online. (2)

   (c) Give **two** advantages to consumers of shopping online. (2)

   (d) Give **one** possible danger to consumers of shopping online. (1)

6.   You have been asked to organise a holiday for yourself and a group of friends. Describe how the Internet could be used to help you plan and book the holiday. (5)

Websites

- Write a brief history of the Internet by using the information at these sites:-
   www.discovery.com/area/history/internet/inet1.html
   www.isoc.org/internet-history
   www.internetvalley.com
   www.w3.org/theproject

- Find out about the latest modem technology by visiting
   www.teleport.com/~curt/modems.html

- "Is all the information on the Internet correct?" Use the article that you'll find at
   www.well.com/user/hir/texts/disinfo.html as a starting point to write an answer to this question.

- Compare the online shopping services offered by these UK supermarkets. Which of the web sites do you think is the best and why?

Tesco	**www.tesco.com**
Sainsbury's	**www.sainsburys.co.uk**

Chapter 20   Web Design Packages

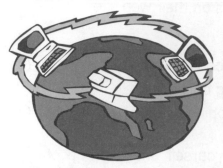

Web pages are created using **Hypertext mark-up language** (**HTML**) which is a fairly simple computer programming language, that tells Web browsers how to display information. Computer users who have no knowledge of HTML can use **Web design packages** to produce individual web pages or complete web sites.

These packages allow pages to be designed in a WYSIWYG environment very similar to that offered by word processing and DTP software to produce printed documents. Once the design process is complete, web design packages automatically convert pages into equivalent HTML code so that they can be viewed on the Internet using Web-browsing software. This chapter describes the features that typical web design packages such as MS FrontPage or Macromedia Dreamweaver offer.

Hyperlinks

Hyperlinks are used to navigate around Web pages. A hyperlink is a piece of text or a graphic that contains the address of another location on the Web. When a user clicks on a hyperlink, they are taken to the location specified in its address. A text hyperlink is normally identified by a distinctive colour, which changes after it has been clicked.

In figure 20.1 below, hyperlinks are used in a Web site to move between pages.

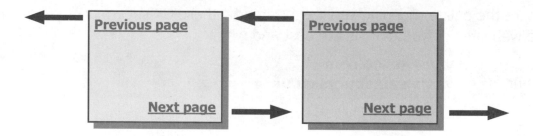

Fig 20.1: Hyperlinks allow users to move around a web site.

The facility to create text or graphical hyperlinks is a basic feature of any Web design package. Without this there would be no way of linking different pages or sections of hypertext together so that users could move around easily within a Web site. Figure 20.2 opposite shows a hyperlink being created.

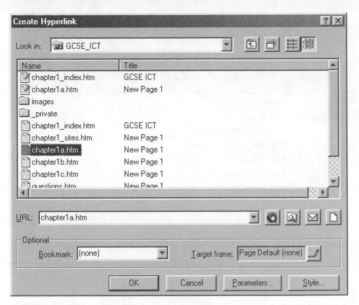

Fig 20.2: Creating a hyperlink.

Hot spots

A hot spot is an area on an object that contains a hyperlink. An object can contain a single hot spot, or multiple hot spots. When a user clicks on a hot spot, they are taken to the location specified in its hyperlink. To create a hot spot an active area must be defined on an object and a hyperlink associated with it. The process of creating a hot spot is described in Figure 20.3 below.

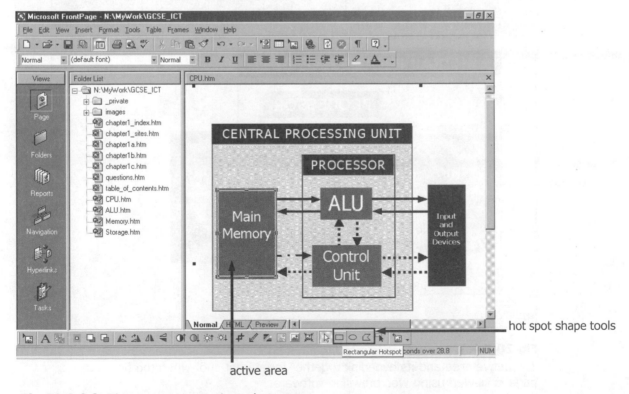

active area

hot spot shape tools

Fig 20.3 (a): The stages in creating a hot spot.
The active area is created by drawing a shape such as a rectangle to define its boundary.

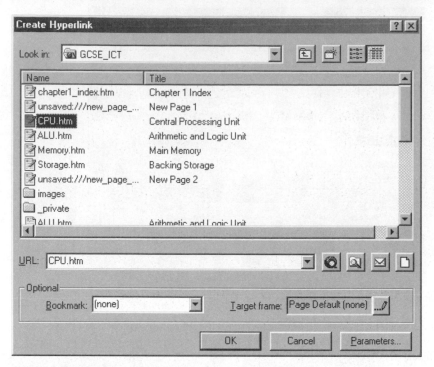

Fig 20.3 (b): The stages in creating a hot spot.
A hyperlink is created and associated with the active area.

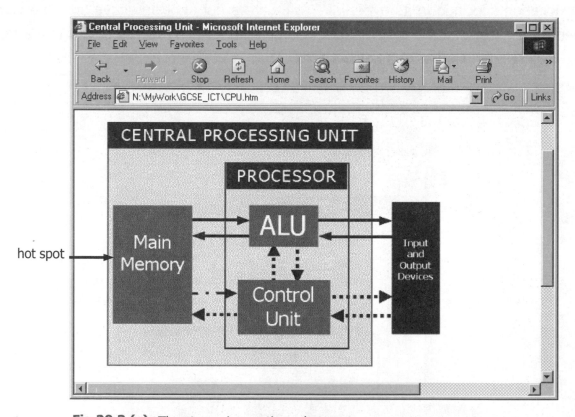

hot spot

Fig 20.3 (c): The stages in creating a hot spot.
The active area and its hyperlink together form a hot spot when the finished
page is viewed using web browsing software.

Tables

Tables can be used to organise and present information on a web page. A table consists of rows and columns of cells, which can be filled with text, colour or graphics. They can help in the creation of more interesting page layouts by allowing text and graphics to be arranged easily.

A good web design package will allow:

- Tables to be created;

- The size of a group of cells or an individual cell to be adjusted;

- Rows and columns to be inserted or deleted;

- Text or other objects within cells to be automatically aligned;

- Cells to be filled with colours, patterns or graphics;

- Different line and border styles around cells.

In Figure 20.4 below a table has been used to organise the text on a web page into a table of contents containing hyperlinks to other pages. This is a common use of tables on Web pages.

Fig 20.4: Using a table to organise the text on a Web page.

Importing text and graphics

A good Web design package will allow text and graphics to be imported, placed on a page and manipulated. Some packages offer more advanced features which allow text or graphics to be animated. Possible sources of images could be clipart on CD-ROM, scanned images, pictures from a digital camera, or graphics from other websites. Text could be from a file created with a word processing application.

Page navigation

It is important that the structure of a web site can be changed so that its pages can be organised into a logical order, which users can navigate their way around easily. A good Web design package will allow the overall structure of a Web site to be viewed and the order of pages to be changed without disrupting the hyperlinks between them. In MS FrontPage for example the structure of a web site is displayed as a tree — as shown in Figure 20.5 below. To change the position of a page it can be 'dragged and dropped' to a new location in the tree.

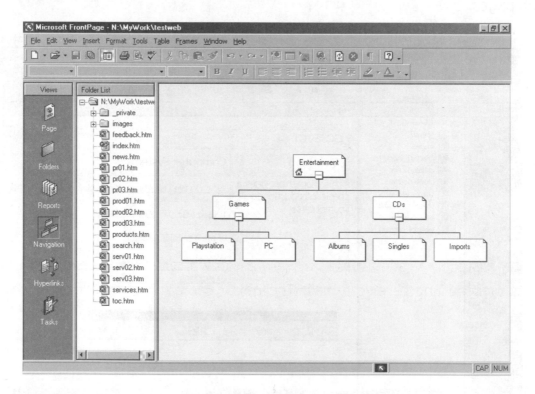

Fig 20.5: Page navigation view in MS FrontPage.

Good Web design

The use of a good Web design package won't necessarily result in the production of a well-designed Web page. The identity of the target audience, contents and overall layout are important factors to consider when planning a Web site. Some basic rules that it can be helpful to follow during the design process are listed below.

- Write clearly and be brief.

- Don't overcrowd pages with large amounts of text and graphics.

- Don't use a lot of graphics — this can make pages take a long time to load.

- Put the most important items at the top of a page — this will attract attention and make people want to look at the rest of the page.

- Use headings and lists to summarise topics so that readers can scan the contents of pages quickly.

- Use bold and italic text to attract attention rather than special effects such as animated or flashing text, which can be annoying.

- Try to make your site easy to navigate by using frames or putting a table of contents at the beginning of a section.

Questions

1. Explain what is meant by the following terms.

   (a) HTML (2)

   (b) Hyperlink (2)

   (c) Hotspot (2)

3. As part of your ICT work at school you have been asked to produce some web pages for the school Intranet.

   (a) Describe **four** features of a web design package that would make this task easier as opposed to writing HTML code. (8)

   (b) Name and give a reason for **three** factors that you would have to take into account when designing the web pages. (6)

3. One of your friends is considering buying a web design package for their PC. Describe **five** essential features that a good web design package should include. Your description must explain how each feature can help users to produce well-designed web pages. (10)

Websites

- Find out more about these popular web design packages:-
  MS FrontPage at http://www.microsoft.com/frontpage/
  Macromedia Dreamweaver at http://www.macromedia.com/software/dreamweaver/productinfo/features/

- Visit www.ncsa.uiuc.edu/general/internet/www/htmlprimer.html to find out about how to use HTML to create a web page.

- Visit www2.hawaii.edu/jay/styleguide for advice on designing and creating your own web site.

Chapter 21

Many businesses are now so dependent on the data that is stored on their computer systems that if it were lost or damaged they would find it very hard to carry on as normal. When data is lost or damaged it is usually due to human error. Sometimes data is damaged deliberately or even stolen. It is important that businesses take steps to protect data from being stolen, lost or damaged. They must also make sure that they can get their data back if anything ever does happen to it. The spread of information communications technology or ICT has resulted in an increase in the misuse of data that is stored electronically.

It is often easier to misuse data stored on a computer rather than in a conventional paper-based system because:-

- Alterations can be made without leaving a trace;

- Very large amounts of data can be stored and searched quickly;

- Data can be instantly transferred to other locations using e-mail and the Internet;

- Communications links used to connect computer systems together are vulnerable to attack from **hackers**. Some hackers create aggressive software that can manipulate or destroy computer programs and data;

- Programs can be designed to deliberately cause damage to computer systems. **Viruses** and **logic bombs** are examples of such programs.

Types of computer crime

Hackers

A hacker is someone who uses their knowledge of computers to break into other computer systems. Hackers use a modem connected to their own computer to 'dial into' the system that they are attacking. Many hackers do this simply because they enjoy the challenge. Once they've broken into another computer system they just leave harmless messages to show that they've been there.

Some hackers are however not so easily satisfied and will deliberately try to cause damage to the computer system that they have broken into. They will often try to do this by deleting important files. To try and control hacking the UK government introduced a law called **The Computer Misuse Act** which made hacking illegal.

Viruses

A virus is a program that can make copies of itself in order to 'infect' other computers. A virus attaches itself to a program or file and then copies itself into other programs and files with which it comes in contact. When a virus runs it may do no real damage or it can do something really nasty such as re-format a hard drive. What a virus does depends on the amount of damage the virus writer wants it to cause. Viruses can spread from one computer to another by way of infected disks, files downloaded from the internet and e-mail. Figure 21.1 below shows how a virus can be passed from one computer to another.

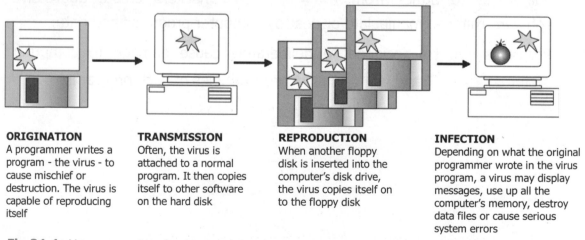

ORIGINATION
A programmer writes a program - the virus - to cause mischief or destruction. The virus is capable of reproducing itself

TRANSMISSION
Often, the virus is attached to a normal program. It then copies itself to other software on the hard disk

REPRODUCTION
When another floppy disk is inserted into the computer's disk drive, the virus copies itself on to the floppy disk

INFECTION
Depending on what the original programmer wrote in the virus program, a virus may display messages, use up all the computer's memory, destroy data files or cause serious system errors

Fig 21.1: How computer viruses are spread.

There are many different types of computer virus but one of the most common types is the 'macro virus'. A macro virus uses the built-in macro language available in most common word processing, spreadsheet and database applications. It gets onto a computer system by attaching itself to a template file, document or e-mail and then running when the file is opened or closed. Macro viruses are a big problem on the Internet with over 1000 different types in existence. The reason that macro viruses are such a problem is that they can be written very easily and infected documents are rapidly transferred to other computer systems.

Virus-scanning software can be used to protect computer systems from infection by viruses. They do this by looking for the unique 'footprints' of known viruses. Every virus infects a computer system in its own special way and leaves tell-tale signs of its presence. These clues are known as the viruses 'footprint'. When a virus scanner detects a virus footprint it deactivates and removes the virus from the computer system.

Most virus-scanning software can be set up to scan files when they are opened, downloaded from the Internet or copied. The main problem with any virus scanner is keeping its list of known viruses up-to-date as lots of new viruses appear every day. For virus-scanning programs to be effective their list of known viruses needs to be updated at least once every six months.

Fig 21.2: Setting virus-scanning software to protect a computer.

Logic bombs

A **logic bomb** is a set of instructions written in computer code that can be hidden inside other software and set to activate at a particular date and time. Once activated a logic bomb will take control of a computer and begin damaging or even deleting data files. Criminals use this type of threat to blackmail businesses into giving them money by claiming they have planted a logic bomb and demanding money to call off the attack.

Software piracy

The theft of software, or software piracy, is a big problem for companies who produce computer software. Software piracy is when illegal copies of software are made to sell or use without paying the company who originally produced the software. The process of developing and testing new software before it is released is very expensive and software piracy costs companies a lot of money from lost sales. In the UK **copyright law** makes it illegal to make extra copies of software to either use or sell without permission.

Security and integrity of data

It is important to know the difference between the **security** of data and the **integrity** of data. When we talk about the security of data we mean keeping it safe from anything that could harm it. Possible dangers include :-

- Natural hazards such as fires, floods or lightning;
- Human error causing loss or damage to data;
- Theft of data electronically due to hacking;
- Physical theft of disks or other computer hardware.

The security of data is concerned with taking steps to avoid any harm to data from these dangers.

The integrity of data is to do with its 'correctness'. It is important that data on computer systems is kept up-to-date and correct. Verification and validation are both ways that we check data is correct. Some of the different measures that can be taken to protect data are described in the rest of this chapter.

Backup copies

Backup copies are kept so that if data is lost, stolen or damaged it can be restored to its original condition. Backup copies should always be kept in a secure, airtight and heatproof container at a location remote from the computers that the data is normally kept on. This is so that if data is lost due to some natural disaster like a fire or flood the backup copies will still be safe. It is also important to make backup copies of data regularly. If backup copies aren't made often enough it will be impossible to restore the data to its original condition. When backups are being made on a network it is normal to backup just the users' data files at the end of every day and all the programs and users' data files at least once a week. This is because the users' data changes more often than the programs on the network and backing up everything can take a lot of time.

Passwords and levels of access

Passwords are often used to restrict access to data on computer systems. Some software packages allow users to **password protect** individual data files. This stops anyone who doesn't know the correct password from opening a file. Figure 21.3 shows a document created using a word processing package being password protected.

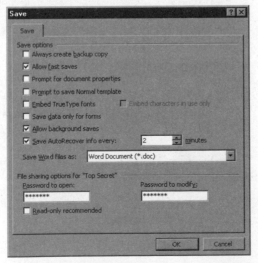

Fig 21.3: Protecting a word processed document with a password.

Some password systems are **hierarchical**. This means that different passwords will give different **levels of access** to data. At the lowest level of access a password will allow just **read-only** access to some data. Read-only access means that data can be used but not changed. The next level of access might be one that allows **read-write** access to some data. Read-write access means that data can be used and changed. The highest possible level of access is a password that allows access to read, change or even delete data anywhere on a computer system. Normally only a small number of people will have this level of access. The type of user who would have this level of access would be someone like a system administrator.

Log files

A log file can be used to help track down people who have stolen or caused damage to data on a computer system. A log file records every attempt to log on to a computer whether or not it was successful. The user identity and attempted time of log-on will be stored in the log file. If a log-on is successful a log file will keep a record of all the files that a user has accessed and the time of any changes that are made. If someone is trying to hack into a system by dialling-in using a modem some log files will keep a record of the telephone number.

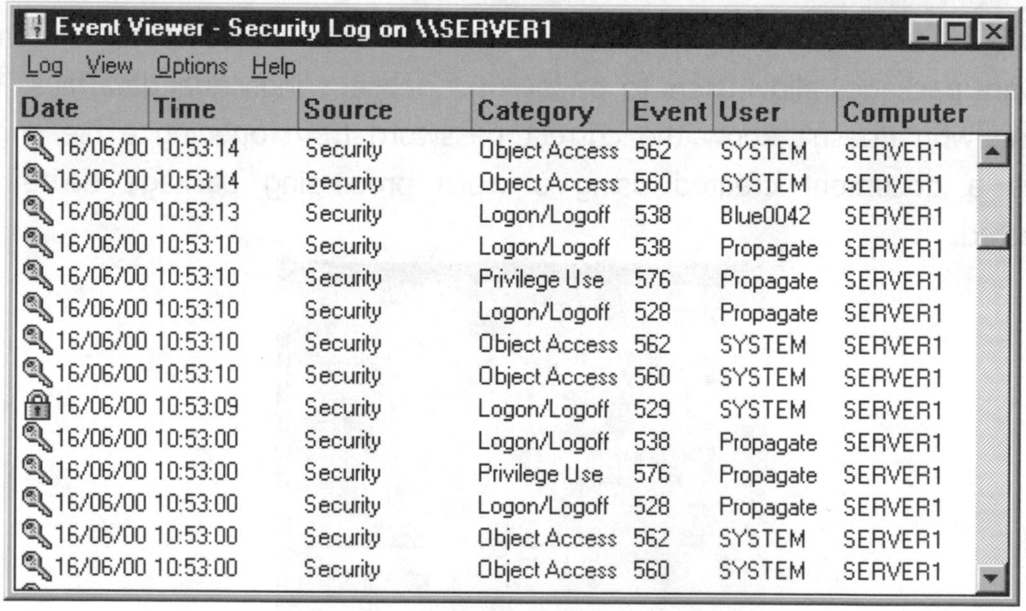

Date	Time	Source	Category	Event	User	Computer
16/06/00	10:53:14	Security	Object Access	562	SYSTEM	SERVER1
16/06/00	10:53:14	Security	Object Access	560	SYSTEM	SERVER1
16/06/00	10:53:13	Security	Logon/Logoff	538	Blue0042	SERVER1
16/06/00	10:53:10	Security	Logon/Logoff	538	Propagate	SERVER1
16/06/00	10:53:10	Security	Privilege Use	576	Propagate	SERVER1
16/06/00	10:53:10	Security	Logon/Logoff	528	Propagate	SERVER1
16/06/00	10:53:10	Security	Object Access	562	SYSTEM	SERVER1
16/06/00	10:53:10	Security	Object Access	560	SYSTEM	SERVER1
16/06/00	10:53:09	Security	Logon/Logoff	529	SYSTEM	SERVER1
16/06/00	10:53:00	Security	Logon/Logoff	538	Propagate	SERVER1
16/06/00	10:53:00	Security	Privilege Use	576	Propagate	SERVER1
16/06/00	10:53:00	Security	Logon/Logoff	528	Propagate	SERVER1
16/06/00	10:53:00	Security	Object Access	562	SYSTEM	SERVER1
16/06/00	10:53:00	Security	Object Access	560	SYSTEM	SERVER1

Fig 21.4: Part of a network security log file.

Physical security measures

Physical security is all about protecting data by restricting access to the computers that the data is being stored on. This is usually done by locking computer rooms and controlling access to them. Access to rooms can be controlled by putting special keypad locks on doors so that a code number must be entered before the lock will be released. Some systems use key cards with magnetic stripes on them which have to be swiped through a magnetic stripe reader at the side of the door before the lock will be released.

Encryption

Encryption is a way of protecting data files that contain sensitive information from being used if they are stolen. **Encrypted data** is coded in such a way that it can't be read unless special decoding, or **decryption**, software is used. Encryption is often used on the Internet to protect data when it is being sent from one computer to another. If someone is buying something on a secure web site their credit card details are encrypted before being transmitted. This is to stop other Internet users from intercepting the data and using it.

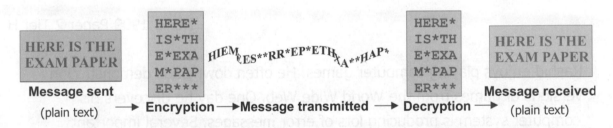

Fig 21.5: Encrypting data.

Questions

1. (a) Explain how the copyright law applies to computer software. (2)

   (b) What is a **hacker**? (1)

   (c) What dangers do hackers present to other computer users? (2)

   NEAB 1999 Paper 1 Tier H

2. Give **three** reasons why it might be easier to misuse personal information stored on computer files rather than the same information stored on paper files. (6)

   NEAB 1995 Paper 1 Tier R

3. In a medical centre, data about the patients is stored on the hard disk of the network file-server.

   (a) Give **two** physical precautions that could be taken to keep the data secure. (2)

   (b) Doctors need to see all the information about patients. Receptionists only need to see some of the information about patients. Describe **one** way in which software could be used to restrict access to patient information. (2)

   NEAB 1999 Paper 2 Tier H

4. Rashid enjoys playing computer games. He often downloads demonstration versions of games from the World Wide Web. One day he discovers his computer system is producing lots of error messages. Several important data files have disappeared. His computer has a virus.

   (a) What is a computer virus? (2)

   (b) Suggest how the virus may have got into Rashid's computer system. (2)

   (c) How can Rashid remove the virus from his computer system? (1)

   (d) What precaution can Rashid take to help prevent more viruses getting into his computer system? (1)

Websites

- Use the information at
  http://jaring.nmhu.edu/notes/security.htm
  http://bsuvc.bsu.edu/~00bwbrown/paper1.html
  to write an article on computer crime and its effects.

- Write a summary of the computer crime case study that you will find at
  http://199.111.112.137/others/seminar/notes/crime2.html

- For links to a variety of other computer crime related web sites visit
  http://cs.selu.edu/~lewismat/ccrime.html

Chapter 22 | The Data Protection Act

Information Technology can be used to collect and store vast amounts of data. Fast processing can quickly turn data into useful information which can be transmitted and shared between ICT systems.

Personal data relates to living, identifiable individuals. It need not be particularly sensitive and can be as little as name and address. The ease with which this data can be transferred electronically from one ICT system to another means that special laws are needed to protect individuals from its misuse. Data that is incorrect, out of date, or becomes confused with someone else's can cause problems. For example, you could be mixed up with another person and turned down for a job or even wrongly arrested. You might be unfairly refused credit or denied social security benefits.

In the United Kingdom a law called **The Data Protection Act** sets out rules for collecting, storing and processing personal data. It applies to paper records as well as those stored on computers. The Data Protection Act first became law in 1984 and was updated in 1998. The new Act came into force on 1 March 2000 and describes:-

- The rules that **data controllers** must follow;

- The rights of **data subjects**;

- The exemptions that exist to the Act.

Data controllers are the people and organisations who store and process personal data; the individuals that the data is about are data subjects.

Rules that data controllers must follow

Data controllers must obey eight principles of 'good information handling' which state that personal data must be:

1. processed fairly and lawfully ;
2. processed for limited purposes;
3. adequate, relevant and not excessive;
4. accurate;
5. not kept longer than necessary;
6. processed in accordance with the data subject's rights;
7. kept secure;
8. not transferred to countries without adequate protection.

Rights of data subjects

If a data subject wants to find out what information is held about them the Data Protection Act allows a 'right of subject access'. The data subject must write to the person or organisation that they believe holds the information and ask for a copy of all the data held about them to which the Data Protection Act applies.

Data subjects can normally see all of the data held about them but there are some exceptions if providing the information would be likely to affect:

- The way crime is detected or prevented;

- Catching or prosecuting offenders;

- Assessing or collecting taxes or duty;

- The right to see certain health and social work details may also be limited.

The copy of the data can be sent as a computer printout, in a letter, or on a form. It must be easy to understand and must include a description of why the data is processed and anyone it may be passed to or seen by.

An example of a letter that could be used is shown below.

> *Dear Sir or madam,*
>
> *Please send me the information that I am entitled to under section 7(1) of the Data Protection Act 1998. If you need further information from me, or a fee, please let me know as soon as possible.*
>
> *If you do not normally handle these requests for your organisation, please pass this letter to your Data Protection Officer or another appropriate official.*
>
> *Yours faithfully,*

Data controllers should reply within 40 days as long as the data subject has provided sufficient proof of their identity and paid any necessary fee, which must not be more than £10. If a reply is not received within 40 days, the organisation should be sent a reminder by recorded delivery. If they still don't reply or if the data received is wrong or incomplete, The Data Protection Commissioner can help make sure that the data subject gets a reply. If one of the principles of good information handling has been broken, she can take action against the data controller to put things right.

Exemptions to the Act

Exemptions are possible for:

- Maintenance of a public register
- Some not-for-profit organisations
- Processing personal data for personal, family or household affairs (including recreational purposes)
- If you only process personal data for
    - staff administration
    - advertising, marketing and public relations
    - accounts and records
- Individuals who are processing personal data for personal, family or household affairs are exempt from notification and most of the other provisions of the Data Protection Act 1998.

The Data Protection Commissioner

The **Data Protection Commissioner** is an independent officer appointed by the Queen who reports directly to Parliament and oversees the implementation of the Data Protection Act. The duties of the Commissioner include: -

- Maintaining a register of the names and addresses of all data controllers who have told the Commissioner that they process personal information. This register describes:
    — the type of data that is being processed;
    — what the data will be used for;
    — the people that the data might be given to;
    — whether the data will be transferred to any countries outside Europe.

- Considering complaints from data subjects about data controllers who have not followed the principles of information handling and prosecuting or serving notices on offenders.

Questions

1. A doctor's surgery stores personal data about its patients on a computer system.

    (a) Give **three** items of personal data, other than name, address and telephone number, that you would expect the surgery to store about patients. (3)

    (b) Describe the steps that the surgery should take to ensure that it complies with the Data Protection Act. (5)

    (c) Some of the patients have objected to data being stored about them on the computer and demanded to see it. Do they have an automatic right to see this data? (2)

2. For each one of the organisations listed below give **two** items of personal data, other than name, address and telephone number, that you would expect them to store about individuals.

    (a) credit reference agency

    (b) telephone company

    (c) employer

    (d) bank or building society

    (e) tax office

    (f) driver and vehicle licensing authority (DVLA) (12)

3. (a) Who or what is the **'Data Protection Commissioner'** ? (2)

    (b) Describe **three** duties that the Data Protection Commissioner performs. (6)

4. Explain how you should go about getting a copy of the personal data held about you by an organisation on its computer system. (3)

5. Mail order companies store personal data about their customers on computer files. The Data Protection Act is designed to protect customers from data misuse.

    (a) Give **three** rights that this Act gives to the customer. (3)

    (b) Give **five** requirements concerning data that the company must meet to comply with the Act. (5)

    (c) Some data is not covered by the Data Protection Act. Name **one** category of data which is granted complete exemption from the Act. (1)

    NEAB 1995 Paper 2 Tier Q

6. Commercial organisations often hold profiles of individuals' personal details on computer databases.

    (a) Give **four** examples of possible sources of the information used to construct these profiles. (4)

    (b) Suggest **two** uses the commercial organisations could make of such profiles. (2)

    (c) Some people are worried about the ethics of the construction and use of such profiles. Discuss the extent to which you think there is a valid concern. (12)

    NEAB 1995 Paper 1 Tier R

Websites

Find out more about the UK Data Protection Act and the activities of the Data Protection Commissioner by visiting the official web site at :

www.dataprotection.gov.uk/dprhome.htm

Computer control is the use of a computer to monitor and control an external process. **Input sensors** are connected to the computer. These sensors are used by the computer to monitor the various parts of a process that it is controlling. Sensors are used to measure changes in the value of some **physical quantity**, such as temperature or light.

Input signals are useless to the computer if it does not know how to interpret them or what actions to take as a result. Before any process can be controlled by a computer a **control program** must be written by a human to tell the computer what to do.

The signals from input sensors are used by the computer to monitor what is going on in the process that it is controlling. Depending upon the value of an input signal from a sensor and the instructions given in its control program, the computer makes a decision about whether an output signal is needed to switch on or off some part of the process's hardware.

Analogue and digital signals

There are two types of input signal which a sensor can send to a computer; these are **digital** and **analogue**. The simplest computer control systems are those which use digital signals. This is because digital signals are easier to process as they can only have two values: **on** (or **true**) and **off** (or **false**). An example of a sensor which sends out a digital signal is an **infra-red sensor**. These are most commonly used by computer-controlled burglar alarms. Infra-red sensors send out an invisible beam of light which is 'broken' when something moves through it. Breaking the beam causes the sensor to send out an 'on' signal to the computer. These digital signals are simple to process because they can be sent directly to the computer which is itself a digital device.

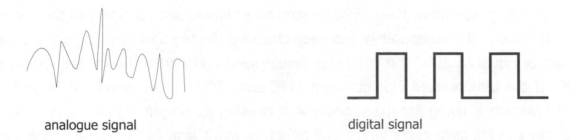

analogue signal   digital signal

Fig 23.1: Analogue and digital signals

Analogue signals are different because they can have any value. A **temperature sensor** is an example of a sensor which sends out analogue signals. Temperature is a physical quantity which can have any number of different values over a given period of time. To be able to process analogue signals sent to it by a sensor the computer needs an **analogue-to-digital** converter or other similar type of **interface** connected to one of its **input ports**. These devices convert the sensor's **analogue signal**, which the computer can't process directly, into an equivalent **digital signal** which the computer can process directly. Figure 23.2 below shows this type of control system.

An analogue signal is sent from the sensor to an analogue-to-digital converter

A digital signal is sent from the analogue-to-digital converter to a computer

Sensor

analogue-to-digital converter

Computer

A sensor detects some physical quantity, such as temperature.

Fig 23.2: Using an analogue-to-digital converter

Feedback

Feedback control systems use the values of their output signals to affect the value of their input signals. Feedback is useful when a certain set of conditions needs to be constantly maintained. Suppose for example that you wanted to use computer control to keep the temperature in your bedroom between 21ºC and 25ºC and you have a heat lamp and a cooling fan connected to your computer. If the temperature was less than 21ºC the computer would send a signal to the heat lamp to turn it on. The computer would keep checking the temperature and once it was greater than or equal to 21ºC the computer would send a signal to the heat lamp to turn it off. If the temperature was more than 25ºC the computer would send a signal to the cooling fan to turn it on. The computer would keep checking the temperature and once it was less than or equal to 25ºC the computer would send a signal to the cooling fan to turn it off. If the temperature was between 21ºC and 25ºC the computer would do nothing. This system is using feedback because it is using its output signals to make changes to the conditions outside which will affect its input signals. The flowchart diagram in Figure 22.3 over the page shows how a feedback control system works.

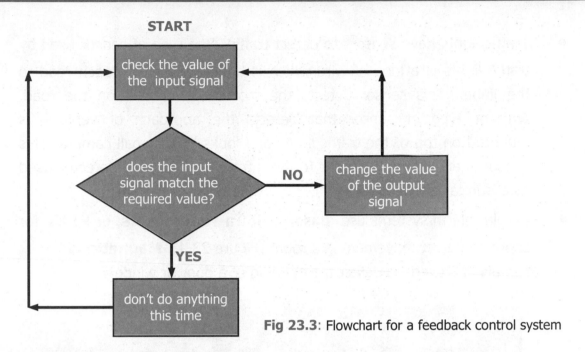

Fig 23.3: Flowchart for a feedback control system

Sensors

The types of sensors used by a computer controlled-system depend upon what sort of process is being controlled. There are many different types of sensor which can each measure some physical quantity outside the computer. Temperature, pressure, light, water and moisture levels, relative humidity, movement and wind speed are just some examples of the physical quantities that sensors can detect. The data that the sensors detect is in the form of analogue data which is converted into digital data before it is sent to the computer. Some common examples of computer-controlled systems and the different types of sensors used by them are described below.

- Many computer-controlled robots use what is known as a **'bump sensor'** to detect when they have struck another object. This can be used to help a robot 'feel' its way around things.

- Computer-controlled greenhouses use **moisture sensors** to detect if the soil is becoming too wet or too dry and **temperature sensors** to detect if the air is too warm or too cold.

- Traffic lights have sensors to detect traffic. One type of sensor used by traffic lights is a loop of wire which is buried in the approach road to the lights. This sensor detects the movement of cars on the road. Another type of sensor that detects the approach of vehicles is mounted on top of the traffic lights and looks like a small camera. This sensor is actually very similar to the infra-red movement detector used by a burglar alarm.

- Burglar alarm systems use **passive infra-red sensors**, or **PIR's** for short, to detect movement in a room (Figure 23.4). **Magnetic catches** can also be used to detect the opening of a door or window.

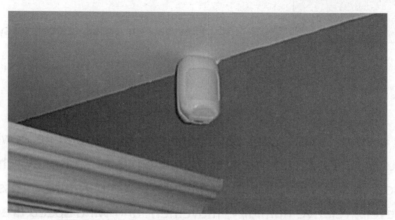

Fig 23.4: Passive infra-red (PIR) sensors are used in burglar alarm systems to detect movement in a room.

Actuators

A computer-controlled system would be useless if it could use sensors to detect what was going on in the outside world but do nothing about it. As we have already seen, computers can send out signals to turn devices like heaters and lights on and off so that they can affect what is going on in the outside world. Many control systems need to control devices that can move such as a motor in a greenhouse to open or close a window. A device called an **actuator** is used to generate signals that can make devices move. Signals are sent from computers to actuators to control the movement of things like hydraulic, pneumatic or motorised systems.

Logo

LOGO is a computer programming language that is often used in education to teach students about computer control. LOGO instructions are used to control the movement of a small shape called a **turtle** around the screen. Figure 23.5 shows a typical LOGO applications package in use.

the lines drawn by turtle as it moves   the **turtle**

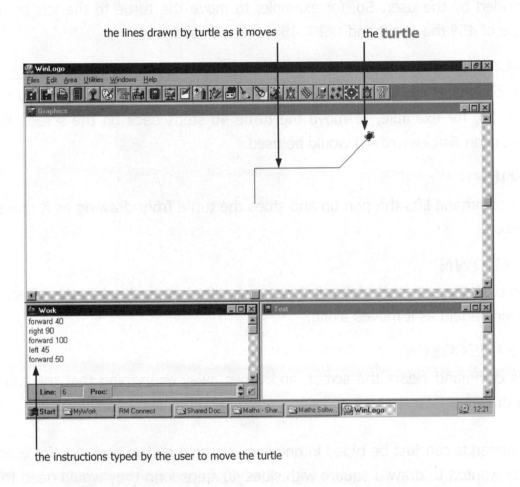

the instructions typed by the user to move the turtle

Fig 23.5: Using LOGO

To make the turtle move on the screen the following commands are used:

FORWARD

This command moves the turtle forward by a number of steps specified by the user. So, for example, to move the turtle 30 steps forward on the screen the instruction **FORWARD 30** would be used.

RIGHT

This command turns the turtle to the right by an angle measured in degrees specified by the user. So, for example, to move the turtle to the right by an angle of 90º the command **RIGHT 90** would be used.

LEFT

This command turns the turtle to the left by an angle measured in degrees specified by the user. So, for example, to move the turtle to the left by an angle of 45º the command **LEFT 45** would be used.

BACKWARD

This command moves the turtle back by a number of steps specified by the user. So, for example, to move the turtle 40 steps back on the screen the instruction **Backward 40** would be used.

PENUP

This command lifts the pen up and stops the turtle from drawing as it moves along.

PENDOWN

This puts the pen back down if it has been lifted up and the turtle will start drawing again as it moves along.

CLEARSCREEN

This command clears the screen and wipes away everything that the turtle has drawn.

LOGO commands can just be typed in one line at a time by the user. So, for example, if the user wanted to draw a square with sides 40 steps long they would need to type in the following instructions one line at a time.

FORWARD 40
RIGHT 90
FORWARD 40
RIGHT 90
FORWARD 40
RIGHT 90

These instructions would draw a square on the screen like the one shown below.

A quicker way to do this would be to use the **REPEAT** command, so the user could type:

REPEAT 4[FORWARD 40 RIGHT 90]

This command would repeat the instructions inside the square brackets four times to build up the sides of the square.

To draw the square without having to type in the same instructions over and over again a **procedure** must be defined. This means that the set of instructions that draw the square are typed in and given a name. Once this has been done the user can tell LOGO to draw the square by typing in just the name of the procedure. To define a procedure to draw the square the user would type in the following:

TO SQUARE
REPEAT 4[FORWARD 40 RIGHT 90]
END

All that the user would have to do to draw the square now would be to simply type the word **SQUARE**. This word could even be used in other instructions or procedures.

Microprocessors

A microprocessor is basically just another name for a CPU. Microprocessors are used to control **automatic machines**. A washing machine is an example of an automatic machine. It is able to follow different wash programs by following pre-programmed sets of instructions, called **control programs** that are stored inside its microprocessor. Automatic machines don't need to be supervised because they are operated by a microprocessor following a control program. Microprocessors can be found around the home inside everyday electrical devices like video recorders, camcorders, hi-fi systems, microwave ovens, dishwashers and burglar alarms.

Fig 23.6: Many everyday household electrical devices contain microprocessors.

Robots

Robots are used in hundreds of applications from assembling and spray-painting cars, carrying out maintenance on overhead power cables, to testing blood samples.

Robots all have the same basic hardware components:

- **sensors** which are used to monitor changes in physical conditions such as speed and position;

- a **microprocessor** to process the information received from sensors;

- **actuators** to produce movement or turn external devices like switches on or off.

Figure 23.7 below shows two robots called Huey and Dewey — named after Donald Duck's nephews, working at a car production plant in the USA. They are applying sealant to stop water leaking into the cars. Huey (top) seals the drip rails while Dewey (right) seals the interior weld seams.

Fig 23.7: Robots assembling a car.
(Photograph courtesy of the Ford Motor Company)

Some of the advantages of robots are:

- They can work in environments that are hazardous to humans, such as in outer space, underwater or in radioactive environments;

- They can perform repetitive and boring tasks without needing to stop for a break;

- The quality of their work is always the same because they never get bored or have an off-day;

- They can work to a greater level of accuracy than humans;

- They can work 24 hours a day, seven days a week, resulting in increased productivity.

The main disadvantage of robots is that they are expensive to buy and install. If a business wants to introduce new production methods or change existing ones it may be easier and cheaper to retrain human workers than replace them with robots.

Questions

1.   Fill in the gaps in the paragraph below using words from the following list.

switch	**light**	**siren**
motor	**controlled**	**validated**
heat	**feedback**	**computers**
pressure	**sensors**	**detect**
switched	**keypads**	**cards**

A building is protected by a computer _____ security system.

_____ are placed at various points in the building to

_____ what is happening.

When it gets dark the outside of the building is lit up by floodlights. A

_____ sensor provides the data needed to operate these.

Underneath the carpet near the doors are _____ sensors. If

someone breaks in a _____ sounds.   (6)

NEAB 1996 Paper 1 Tier P

2.   (a) Explain what is meant by the term **microprocessor**.   (1)
     (b) Name **four** different types of household device that are controlled
         by a microprocessor and explain briefly what the microprocessor
         controls.   (4)

3.   Give **one** suitable type of sensor for each of the computer control applications
     listed below. In each case give one reason for your choice of sensor.

     (i)   Turning a security light on at dusk.
     (ii) Stopping a factory robot from bumping into things.
     (iii) Checking if plants need watering in a greenhouse.
     (iv) Detecting the traffic approaching a pedestrian crossing.
     (v)   Monitoring a baby's temperature in an incubator.
     (vi) Detecting movement in the rooms of a house for a burglar alarm.   (12)

4. The reptile house in a zoo uses a control system to keep conditions stable.

    The reptile house has to be kept between 23°C and 31°C.
    Within the reptile house are heaters and extractor fans.

    (a) What kind of sensor would be required to keep the reptile house
        between 23°C and 31°C? (1)
    (b) Explain how the reptile house would make use of monitoring and
        feedback to keep the reptile house between 23°C and 31°C. (5)

    NEAB 1996 Paper 1 Tier R

5. To help increase security at their home, Mr and Mrs Patel have decided to fit a light to the outside of their house. They want the light to come on when a person approaches the house and it is dark. Light sensors will be fitted to detect when it is dark.

    (a) Give **two different** types of sensor that could be fitted to detect when
        a person approaches. (2)
    (b) Explain why more than one light sensor may be needed. (2)
    (c) Explain why the sensors need to be calibrated to a known scale before
        use. (2)

    NEAB 1998 (Short Course) Tier H

Websites

- Read about how the UK Met. Office uses data logging at:
  www.meto.gov.uk/sec2/pg3/awsintro.html

- For information about the type of data logging equipment that is used to collect weather data visit the Campbell Scientific website at:
  www.campbellsci.co.uk/products/weather/weather.htm
  This site also has some good examples of other ways that data logging has been used.

- For information about data logging software and ideas on how to use data logging in school visit **www.dcpmicro.com/**

Chapter 24 — Health and Safety

Working with computers for long periods of time can cause many different kinds of health problems. These can include stress, eyestrain and injuries to the wrists, neck and back. Employers must take steps to protect employees whose work involves the regular use of computers from these health risks or face the risk of being sued for compensation. This chapter describes these health risks, how they can be avoided or reduced and the obligations that the law places on employers to protect their employees from them.

Stress

Stress brought on through the use of computers is one of the major causes of work-related illness. For some people just the thought of working on a computer can give them stress. A recent survey, commissioned by the technology firm ICL, measured the stress levels of 200 people caused by their use of computers. It asked them how computer faults compared with other stressful situations. According to the study, 68 percent of those surveyed said visiting the in-laws was less stressful than a computer crash and one third said they would rather baby sit!

Some of the ways that ICT systems can cause stress for workers are described below.

- Many people are afraid of computers and fear that they will be left behind or made redundant if they are unable to learn new ICT skills quickly enough and keep up with the younger more computer-literate generation;

- ICT systems make information instantly available wherever you are. Mobile phones, pagers, portable computers and the Internet make it possible to work anywhere. This means that some people find it virtually impossible to forget about work and relax.

- The amount of information that ICT systems can produce is often far too much for anyone to take in. This results in 'information overload', which causes workers to become stressed by the feeling that they can't cope with the information that they are receiving.

- Workers can be monitored using ICT systems — the feeling of being constantly 'watched' caused by this can be very stressful.

Repetitive strain injury

Repeating the same physical movements over and over again can cause a condition known as **Repetitive Strain Injury** (**RSI**). For regular computer users it is the repeated presses on the keyboard and long periods of holding and moving a mouse which cause a build up of damage to the hands and arms and shoulders.

Some of the more common symptoms of RSI are:

- Tightness, aching or stiffness in the arms, neck or shoulders.
- Numbness, coldness, or tingling in the arms and hands;
- Clumsiness or loss of strength in the hands;

Sitting in the correct position, using specially designed furniture, keyboards and wrist rests, and learning how to type correctly can help to avoid RSI or at least reduce the damage that might be caused. Adopting a correct typing technique, for example, includes trying to do the following:

- Don't rest your wrists on anything when you're typing;
- Don't bend your wrists to the side, up or down;
- Keep your wrists in the same position and stretch your fingers to hit keys instead of moving your hands around.

Eyestrain

Spending long periods of time in front of a computer screen can cause eyestrain. This may be experienced as pain in the eyes, watering, blurred or double vision and headaches. Although there is no evidence that eyestrain causes any permanent damage, its symptoms can be very uncomfortable and distressing. Eyestrain can be avoided by making sure that there is enough light in the workplace, reducing the amount of glare from light being reflected off computer screens and making sure that the correct prescription glasses are worn by any workers who need them.

Extremely low frequency (ELF) radiation

We are exposed to extremely low frequency, or ELF, radiation every day from sources such as the sun, the earth's magnetic field and even electricity mains at home and in the workplace. Computer monitors are also a common source of ELF. Some studies have shown that this type of radiation may cause health problems. There is some evidence for example that working for long periods in front of computer screen may increase the risk of a miscarriage during pregnancy.

Computers, health and the law

Laws that are designed to protect people from health hazards in the workplace are administered in the UK by a government body called the **Health and Safety Executive**, or **HSE**. The particular law relating to the use of computer screens is called the **Health and Safety (Display Screen Equipment regulations) 1992**.

This legislation requires employers to:

- Inspect workstations to make sure that they meet the required standards for health and safety;
- Train employees how to use workstations correctly;
- Make sure that employees take regular breaks or changes in activity;
- Provide regular eye tests for workstation users and pay for prescription glasses.

This legislation requires employees to:

- Use workstations and equipment correctly in accordance with the training provided by their employer.
- Inform their employer of any problems relating to Health and Safety as soon as they arise and co-operate with the correction of these problems.

The manufacturers of computer hardware must also make sure that their products comply with this legislation. For example screens must tilt and swivel and keyboards must be separate and moveable.

Workplace design

The health and safety laws relating to the use of computer equipment in the workplace also set minimum standards that furniture and equipment must meet. When purchasing new equipment or designing a working ICT environment, employers must give consideration to:

- **Lighting.**

The workplace should be well lit so that reflected light from computer screens does not cause glare which can lead to eyestrain. Adjustable blinds should be provided at windows. Computers should be positioned so that they do not face or back onto windows.

- **Furniture.**

Height-adjustable swivel chairs with backrests should be provided and positioned at the correct height and distance from the desk and keyboard. Desks should be large enough to hold both the computer and any paperwork. Adjustable document holders must be provided so that awkward repetitive head movements can be avoided when entering data.

- **Noise.**

The work space should be quiet and noisy devices such as dot-matrix printers, for example, should be fitted with acoustic covers or moved to a separate room.

- **Hardware.**

Screens must not flicker and should tilt and swivel. Keyboards must be separate, moveable and fitted with wrist supports.

- **Software.**

Software should make the tasks that employers require employees to perform easier. It must be easy to use and adaptable to the user's experience.

- **The working environment.**

The work space should be well ventilated and maintained at a comfortable temperature and humidity with air conditioning and heating.

Some of the features that a well designed computer workstation should incorporate are shown in Figure 24.1 below.

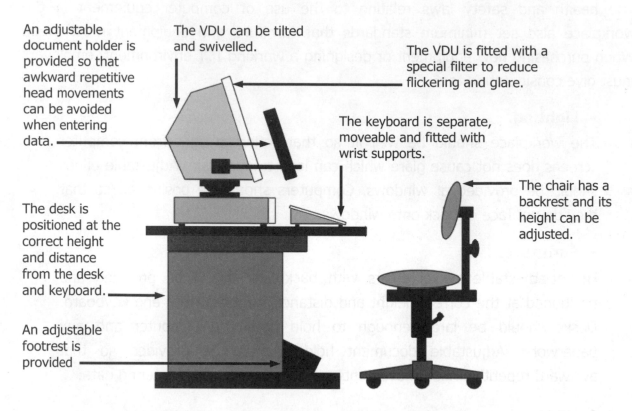

An adjustable document holder is provided so that awkward repetitive head movements can be avoided when entering data.

The VDU can be tilted and swivelled.

The VDU is fitted with a special filter to reduce flickering and glare.

The keyboard is separate, moveable and fitted with wrist supports.

The chair has a backrest and its height can be adjusted.

The desk is positioned at the correct height and distance from the desk and keyboard.

An adjustable footrest is provided

Fig 24.1: A well-designed computer workstation.

Questions

1. The use of computers in the workplace has been linked with a number of possible health hazards.

   (a) Give **three** health hazards that have been linked with the use of computers in the workplace. (3)

   (b) Describe **five** precautions that an employer can take to try and avoid exposing computer operators to these health hazards. (5)

2. Laws that are designed to protect people from health hazards in the workplace are administered in the UK by a government body called the Health and Safety Executive.

   (a) Describe **three** obligations that the law places on employers to protect workers who operate computer terminals from possible health risks. (3)

   (b) Describe **two** obligations that the law places on employees who operate computer terminals to protect themselves from possible health risks. (2)

3. The introduction of computers into the workplace has resulted in a large increase in the number of people forced to take sick leave through stress-related illnesses. Describe how the use of computers at work can be a source of stress for many employees. (8)

4. Describe **five** factors that should be considered when designing a workplace for computer operators. Your answer should pay particular attention to the ways in which a well-designed workplace can help to avoid the health risks that are associated with the prolonged use of computer terminals. (10)

Websites

- Write an article about the health risks of VDUs – use the information on the HSE website at **http://www.hse.gov.uk/pubns/indg36.htm** as a starting point.

- Summarise the information on the PIN website at **http://www.pin.org.uk/learning/health.htm** about health and safety using computer equipment in schools.

ICT in supermarkets

Supermarkets use a computer system called 'electronic point of sale' or EPOS to:

- monitor and control stock by automatically generating orders for more products when the number in stock falls below a certain level;

- perform sales analysis to find out which products are selling well and which ones aren't;

- collect data about customers using loyalty cards which offer points whenever money is spent in the store. This data is used to analyse the spending habits of customers and send them offers for the type of products that they buy regularly.

Supermarket checkouts are called **EPOS terminals**. Each one of these terminals is connected to a minicomputer in the store where a database of product information is stored. This computer is linked to the supermarket chain's mainframe computer using a telecommunications link such as a telephone line or satellite dish. The parts of a typical EPOS terminal are illustrated in Figure 25.1 below.

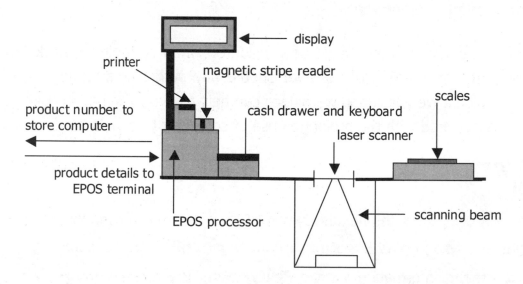

Fig 25.1: The parts of an EPOS terminal.

UK supermarkets use the **European Article Number** or **EAN** barcode system. This uses barcodes to represent a thirteen-digit **EAN number**, which identifies a product, its country of origin and manufacturer. The last digit of an EAN is a check digit which is used to make sure the number has been correctly input (this was explained in Chapter 4). Figure 25.2 below shows the parts of an EAN product barcode.

The first 2 digits identify the country where the product was made. → 50 01935 01432 3 ← The last digit is the check digit.

The next 5 digits identify the manufacturer of the product.

The next 5 digits are the product code.

Fig 25.2: The parts of a EAN barcode.

When a product is sold the following sequence of events takes place:

- a barcode scanner is used to read the EAN number from the product;

- the EAN number is sent to the branch computer by the EPOS terminal;

- the branch computer uses the EAN number to search the stock file for the product's price and description which it sends back to the EPOS terminal;

- the branch computer updates the stock level for the product to show that one has been sold;

- the product's price and description are displayed at the EPOS terminal and printed on a receipt;

- the price of the product is added to the total of the products processed so far.

At the end of every day the branch computer sends its stock level data to a mainframe computer at head office using a telephone line or satellite link. This data is analysed to decide what stock needs delivering to the supermarket the following day. Orders are generated by the mainframe for every branch of the supermarket and sent to regional distribution warehouses where stock is held centrally ready to be loaded onto lorries and delivered direct to the stores.

Some of the advantages of EPOS systems in supermarkets are:

- Shelves are always well stocked, fresh food is readily available and products very rarely run out;

- Customers can be dealt with much more quickly at the checkout;

- Customers receive a fully-itemised receipt;

- Goods can be paid for using electronic funds transfer (EFT) ;

- Accurate and up-to-date sales analysis information is always available for managers;

- Customer buying patterns can be analysed and used to target customers with offers for goods and services that they might be interested in.

The main disadvantages of EPOS systems are that they are expensive to install, require regular maintenance and must be kept up-to-date compared with rival supermarket systems if a competitive edge is to be maintained.

ICT and banks

Automated Teller Machines (ATMs)

Banks use mainframe computers to maintain their customer accounts by dealing with the transactions generated as a result of withdrawals and deposits. Each bank mainframe is also used to operate a network of **automated teller machines** or **ATMs**, which customers can use to gain access to their accounts at any time of the day or night.

Typically, an ATM can be used to:

- withdraw cash;
- check an account balance;
- order a statement or print a 'mini statement';
- order a cheque book.

The parts of an ATM are shown in Figure 25.3 below.

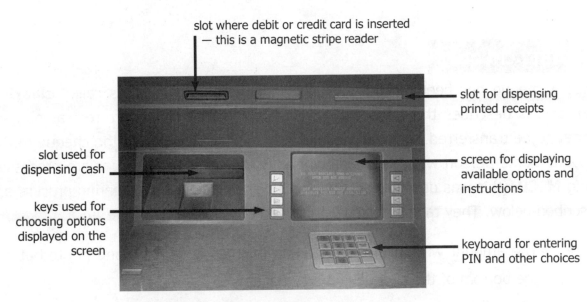

Fig 25.3: The parts of an ATM.

To use an ATM a debit or credit card must be inserted in the machine which reads an account number from the magnetic stripe on the back of the card. The ATM then asks the customer to enter their **personal identification number**, or **PIN**. This is a security measure, which is used to prevent unauthorised access to accounts. The customer is only given three attempts to enter the correct number before the ATM retains the card. If a correct PIN is entered the customer is asked to select the option that they require from an on-screen menu which lists the available choices. If cash is being withdrawn the amount must be entered and the ATM checks the current balance of the customer's account to see if they have enough money. If there are sufficient funds in the account the transaction is authorised, the cash is dispensed and the account balance is updated straight away.

The advantages of ATMs are:

- Banks can keep their operating costs down because fewer employees are needed to work behind the counter inside branches;

- Customers have 24-hour access to their accounts seven days a week;

- There's no need to carry large amount of cash around as the large number of ATMs means that it is readily available.

Clearing cheques

Once a cheque has been written and paid into the bank a process called **clearing** begins; this describes the steps that take place in order for the correct amount of money to be transferred from the account of the person who wrote the cheque to the account of the person whose name is written on the cheque. Cheques are processed using **MICR** (this was described in Chapter 3). The stages of the clearing process are described below. They take between 3-5 days to complete on average.

- The amount written on each cheque is entered by hand and printed at the bottom of the cheque in magnetic ink;

- All of the cheques that have been paid in that day are sent to a central processing centre called a **clearing house**;

- The data printed at the bottom of the cheque in magnetic ink is automatically input by passing the cheques through **magnetic ink character readers**, transferred onto magnetic disk and sorted into bank order. MICR is used because data from large numbers of cheques can be input very quickly and accurately;

- All of the data for each bank is copied onto individual magnetic disks;

- All of the cheques are sorted into bank and branch order and sent back to each bank where they are stored in case there are any problems or enquiries from customers;

- A magnetic disk containing a **transaction file** with details of all the amounts to be added to and deducted from customer accounts is sent to the bank's own computer centre;

- Customer accounts are updated using the transaction file.

Electronic funds transfer (EFT)

All banks offer their customers the use of a **debit card** facility. **SWITCH** and **DELTA** are the two main types of debit card in the UK. These cards can be used to pay for goods and services instead of cash or cheques. This type of payment system is called **electronic funds transfer** or just **EFT** for short; its main advantages are that bank accounts are updated straight away and there's no need to use cash or wait for cheques to clear. Suppose, for example, you were paying for a CD in a music store using a debit card. Your card would be swiped through a magnetic stripe reader and your bank's computer would be contacted to make sure there was enough money in your account to pay for the CD. Provided that the funds were available, the payment would be authorised and the money would be exchanged electronically between the shop's computer and your bank account.

Smart cards

A smart card looks exactly like a credit or debit card except that it has a microchip built into it (Figure 25.4) which can be used to store much more data than a magnetic stripe more reliably and securely. Money is transferred directly from the customer's bank account using special telephones or ATMs and stored on the card inside an electronic purse. To use the card it must be unlocked using a PIN number. Retailers have a special terminal which has their own smart card inside. When goods or services are purchased the customer's card is placed in the terminal and money is transferred from one card to another.

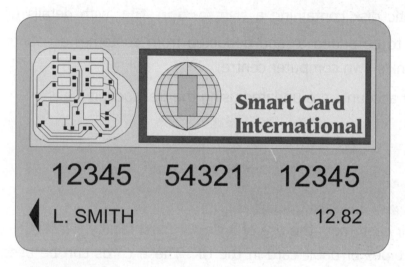

Fig 25.4: A smart card — the microchip is in the top left hand corner of the card.
Reproduced from Computer Desktop Encyclopædia with permission.
(c) 1981-2000 The Computer Language Co. Inc., www.computerlanguage.com

The main advantages of smart cards are:

- They can be used just like cash without the need to wait for authorisation like EFT systems;

- Smart card technology is more reliable than magnetic stripes which are easily damaged;

- Smart cards offer better security than magnetic stripe cards because they are much more difficult to forge and generate a unique digital code each time they are used;

- A single smart card can be used for a number of different applications such as:
  - holding an electronic purse;
  - being used as a credit card;
  - being used as an identity card;
  - being used as an electronic key to open doors that have been fitted with locks that have smart card readers fitted;
  - being used on holiday by holding foreign currencies in extra electronic purses.

ICT and medicine

Body scanners

One common use of ICT in medicine is the use of body scanners. A body scanner sends electromagnetic rays through a patient's body and sensors detect how much different parts of the body absorb the rays. A computer uses this data to build up an image of the inside of a patient's body, this can be a cross-section or even three-dimensional. Before body scanners the only way to find out what was happening inside the body was to operate on the patient. Body scanners allow doctors to find and treat conditions such as tumours in their early stages when the chances of treating them successfully are much greater.

Patient monitoring

Computers are used in hospitals to monitor critically ill patients in intensive care units. The patient has sensors attached to him which detect changes in heart rate, pulse rate, blood pressure, breathing and brain activity. If any of these fall below a preset level the computer sounds an alarm and alerts the medical staff. The data is also logged and used to analyse the changes in a patient's condition over a period of time.

Organ transplants

Computerised databases are used to help match patients who are waiting for organ transplants such as a new kidney, liver or heart, with suitable organs from donors. A database is used to store details about patients such as their tissue and blood types. This data is compared with information about organs as they become available for transplant to try and match patients to the most compatible donor organ.

Patient records

Computerised databases are used by every hospital in the country to store information about patients. Storing information in this way makes it much more easily available and means that paper-based records are not constantly following patients around the hospital. If a patient is based on one ward but being seen by a consultant and receiving treatment in other parts of the hospital their details can be viewed and updated at any terminal on the hospital's local area network.

The type of information stored about each patient includes their address, the name of their GP, their religion, their occupation and employment details, medical history, details of past and present medication, and emergency contact details. These databases have many uses in a hospital besides looking up a patient's medical history, these include:

- organising the transfer of patients between wards;
- recording the history of a patient's appointments with a consultant;
- booking outpatient appointments;
- booking ambulances;
- ordering equipment.

Questions

1. (a) What do the letters **EPOS** stand for? (1)
   (b) Explain how a supermarket uses EPOS to keep the shelves well stocked with goods. (3)
   (c) Draw and label a diagram of an EPOS terminal. (6)

2. (a) Describe **two** input methods used at a supermarket EPOS terminal. (2)
   (b) Give two output devices that would be connected to an EPOS terminal. (2)
   (c) Supermarket EPOS terminals are connected to the store computer. Explain why this is necessary. (2)
   (d) Describe **one** other way that supermarkets use computers. (2)

3. (a) What do the letters **EFT** stand for? (1)
   (b) Give one method of input used by an EFT system. (1)
   (c) Give two advantages of using an EFT system. (2)
   (d) Give **one** disadvantage of EFT.

4. Many banks are now experimenting with smart card technology.
   (a) What is a **smart card**? (2)
   (b) Give **three** advantages of smart cards compared with traditional magnetic stripe card technology. (3)
   (c) Do you believe that the use of smart cards will lead to a completely 'cashless' society? (5)

5. Every bank in the country has a network of cash machines, or ATMs.
   (a) Give **two** input devices used at an ATM. (2)
   (b) Give **two** output devices used at an ATM. (2)
   (c) To use an ATM a customer needs a debit or credit card and a PIN.
      (i) What do the letters PIN stand for? (1)
      (ii) Explain why a PIN is needed. (1)
   (d) Give **three** services, other than withdrawing cash and checking account balances, that you would expect a typical ATM to offer customers. (3)

Websites

- Read Reynolds Griffith's article "Cashless Society or Digital Cash?" at:

  www.sfasu.edu/finance/FINCASH.HTM

  and write your own argument about whether we will ever have a truly 'cashless' society and the impact this might have on our lives. You may also find these links useful:

  www.networkusa.org/fingerprint/page5a/fp-05a-page5a-cashless.html

  www.heise.de/tp/english/special/eco/6093/1.html
  www.netspace.net.au/~newdawn/33b.htm

- Visit **http://pigseye.kennesaw.edu/~afowler1/** for a description of some of the uses of computers in medicine.

60% of the marks for AQA (NEAB) full course GCSE Information and Communication Technology (Specification A) come from coursework, which consists of:

- a Board-set assignment worth 30%;
- a project worth 30%.

NB For the short course you will only need to complete the Board-set assignment.

This section gives some guidelines on how to improve your coursework marks by making sure that the written reports you produce contain all of the necessary evidence organised into the correct order.

Board-set assignment

The Board-set assignment will consist of a description of a situation where ICT can be used to solve some problems. You will have to produce a report that describes what the problems are and design, implement, test and evaluate solutions to them. You will receive a booklet that contains a description of the situation that the assignment is based upon. You must use the information in this booklet to:

- Carry out an **analysis** to identify the tasks that need to be completed.

  For each task you must:
  — Describe the outputs that are needed;
  — Describe some possible ways of solving the problem;
  — Choose the best solution and give reasons for your choice;
  — Describe exactly what the solution must do;
  — Describe the evidence that you will need to produce in order to prove that solution does what is required and has been successfully completed.

  Once you have completed the analysis your teacher will mark it. You may not have identified all of the tasks or got them in the right order. Don't worry about this — your teacher can tell you what each task is at this stage and how they should be numbered.

- Produce a **design** for each task, which must describe:
  - What the solution must do in terms of the input, processing and output that is needed;
  - The hardware and software that you will use to solve the problem giving reasons for your choices;
  - The tests that you will carry out to prove you have successfully solved the problem. The best way to do this is to write a test plan (as described in Chapter 16).

    Some solutions may not need testing — your teacher will help you to decide if this is the case if you aren't sure.

- Produce evidence of **implementation** for each task, which must describe:

  How you went about solving each problem and the features of the software that you have used. Include printouts that show the stages you went through as you developed the solution. Try to write some brief comments on printouts to explain what they show. If a printout doesn't show anything useful don't include it!

  Some tasks might not require any implementation — your teacher can help you to decide if this is the case when you are designing solutions to the problems.

- Produce evidence that you have **tested** the solution for a task by following its test plan. You must include printouts for every test in the test plan and write comments on them to explain what was being tested and whether the expected result was obtained. You should also describe any changes that you made if a test showed that something didn't work.

- Produce an **evaluation** of the solutions that you have produced for the tasks.

  Describe how successful each solution was by answering questions like:
    - What was the solution supposed to do (refer to your analysis and design sections);
    - Did the solution solve the problem and do exactly what was required?
    - Did you need to make any changes to the solution after you had tested it? If so, what did you do and did it work?

  You might not need to evaluate every solution — check this with your teacher.

Project

For the project you will have to produce a report on an investigation into a problem that you have designed and developed a solution for. Your teacher will tell you about the types of problems that are suitable but in the end the choice is yours.

To get the best possible marks for your project you should try to:

- Come up with a situation that is real — don't just make something up!

- Identify a situation where a small number of different problems need solving — don't just concentrate on producing a solution to a single problem.

- Produce solutions to problems that can be used by real people after you have finished them.

You must write a report about your project — the things that you need to include in this are described on the next few pages.

Analysis

During this stage of your project work you are taking on the role of a systems analyst by trying to identify and investigate the problems with the existing system. Remember there are different ways of gathering information about a system such as using questionnaires, interviewing people and examining paperwork (these were described in Chapter 16) — you don't have to do all of these things but it will help you to produce a better project if you do some of them.

- Describe the background to the situation that you have chosen for your project work —— do this by answering questions like:
  - Who will you be trying to solve problems for?
  - Is it a business or an individual?
  - What sort of work do they do?
  - What services do they provide?

- Describe the problems that there are with the existing system —— do this by answering questions like:
  - What is being done, how is it being done and who is doing it?
  - What problems are there with how things are being done now?
  - Which of these problems are the most important and need solving straight away?
  - Can any of the problems be broken down into smaller problems? If so what are they?

- Decide which of the problems that you have identified are the ones that you're going to try and solve. Remember your time is limited so don't try and do everything. List these problems clearly and in order of their importance. For each of these problems you should:
  - Describe possible ways of solving the problem.
  - Describe the way that you are going to solve the problem and explain the reasons for your decision.
  - Describe the things that your solution must do for it to be judged as having been successful.

Design

You need to produce a detailed design for each problem by considering and producing answers to questions like:

- What software will you need to use?
    - Which types of application packages are you going to use?
    - Why are these types of packages the most suitable?
    - Which specific package will you be using and why?

        e.g. You might say that you need to use a database package and could use either MS Access or Lotus Approach. You should discuss the features that these packages offer which could be used to solve the problem and explain which one you've decided to use and why. Remember to consider what software the person who'll be using the finished system has access to — this could influence your decision.

- What hardware will you need to use?
    You must consider what type of computer is needed to be able to use the software that you have chosen:
    - What type of operating system is required? (e.g. Windows 98, MacOS)
    - What minimum type of processor is required? (e.g. Celeron 250, Pentium II 400)
    - How much hard disk space is needed? (e.g. 300 Mb minimum free space)
    - How much RAM is needed? (e.g. 64 Mb)
    - Is a CD-ROM drive required?
    - What type of printer is needed? (e.g. inkjet, laser or dot-matrix)
    - Are any other peripheral devices needed? (e.g. scanner)

- What data will need to be input, where will it come from and how will it be input?
- What will any input screens need to look like and have on them?
- What output is required from the system?
- What output methods will be used?

- What layout is needed on printed output?

- What will output screens need to look like and have on them?

- If the solution to a problem involves creating a database you should decide what data files are needed and produce a file design that describes exactly what sort of data each record in the file will need to store.

  e.g. If you were creating a database to help run a video shop you would probably need data files to store information about videos, members and videos on loan.

  For each data file you should produce a file design like the one shown in the example below .

Design for the *Video* file

Field Name	Data Type	Length	Format	Validation
Video Number	Numeric	3 digits	Integer	Must be greater than 0 and less
Title	Text	30 characters	None	Can have any value
Certificate	Text	2 characters	Coded	Must be one of: U, PG, 12, 15, 18
Category	Text	3 characters	Coded	Must be one of:

- If the solution to a problem involves creating a spreadsheet you should decide what layout is needed and produce a design that shows this along with the cell formats, data formats and formulae that will be needed.

- You must describe the tests that you will carry out to show that the solution works correctly; do this by producing a test plan as shown in the table below (an example of a test plan appears in Chapter 16).

Test Nº	Purpose	Test Data	Expected Result

Implementation

This section is where you must provide evidence of the work that you have done. You should try to produce 'screen shots' and other printouts showing the stages you have worked through in developing the solution to a problem. Write comments on printouts to explain what they show and describe the features of the software that is being used.

Testing

You must follow the test plan for each problem and make a record of the results obtained for each test. As far as possible try to produce printed evidence of test results and make sure that any printouts have the test number written on them along with a comment explaining what was being tested, whether the test was successful and any further action that is necessary. You should write an overall evaluation of the test results that compares what actually happened with what was expected to happen. It is also important that you describe any changes that had to be made to the system in order to solve problems found during testing.

Evaluation

You must evaluate how successful your solution to each problem was by comparing what you actually produced with what you said a successful solution should be able to do, back in the analysis section of your report.

User Guide

You must produce a user guide that describes how to use the solution to a problem. A good user guide describes how to use a system and shouldn't just describe how to use a particular software package. A user guide should contain the following items:

- a description of what the system is designed to do;
- minimum hardware and software requirements of the system;
- instructions on how to load and run the system;
- detailed instructions on how to operate each part of the system;
- error messages, their meaning and how to deal with them;
- where to get more help, such as telephone support lines and on-line tutorials.

This summary of subject content is for the AQA (NEAB) full course in GCSE Information and Communication Technology (Specification A) and is valid for examinations from 2003 onwards. The highlighted sections are **not** covered by the short course. Up to date information and syllabus support materials can be found at the AQA Web site at **http://www.aqa.org.uk**

Topic	Amplification	See Chapter
9.2 Hardware components	Understand what a range of hardware is capable of and its usefulness in an information system. Details of operation are not required.	
Input peripherals	Input peripherals expected are:	2
	• Keyboard, including specialised keyboards	
	• Mouse, touch pad, tracker ball, joystick	
	• Graphics digitiser	
	• Touch-sensitive screen	
	• Light pen	
	• Scanner, digital camera for photographs or video	
	• Microphone	
	• Sensor	23
Output peripherals	Output peripherals expected are:	6
	• Screen (VDU)	
	• Printers (dot-matrix, laser, inkjet)	
	• Plotters	
	• Speakers	
	• Motors and switched output in control systems	23
Storage devices and media	Storage devices and media expected are:	5
	• ROM, RAM	
	• Hard and floppy disks	
	• Magnetic tape	
	• CD-ROM, CD-Recordable, CD-Rewritable	
	• DVD ROM, DVD RAM	
	• Know the difference between them in terms of whether they are volatile or not and their uses.	

	Topic	Amplification	See Chapter
9.3	**Operating environment**		
	The role of operating systems	Know that the operating system: Provides a means of communication between applications software and the hardware of the computer system; Manages system resources including memory and allocation of CPU time; Manages data transfers including transfers to and from peripherals; Manages system security.	**7**
	Types of operating systems	Show awareness that different operating systems exist and be able to describe the special facilities needed in multi-tasking and multi-user systems. Understand that applications software may be specific to a particular operating system.	
9.4	**Data transfer**	Know that transfer of data files in graphics, text, sound or numeric format is possible between applications, packages and machines. Know that the use of standard file formats makes such transfer easier (details of file formats are not required).	**1, 14**
9.5	**User interface**	Understand that interfaces can be command-driven, menu-driven or graphical. Discuss the advantages and disadvantages of these types of interface for different categories of users. Identify design considerations in developing a user interface for a particular purpose including consistency, positioning of items on the screen, use of colour, use of sound and availability of help.	**8**
9.6	**Applications software**		
	The function of applications software within the system	Know that applications software is designed to carry out user-related tasks.	**9**
	The types of applications software used.	Know when software is suitable for a given task and understand the purpose of, and have experienced the use of, software covering the facilities and the techniques detailed below: *Note: It is the facilities and processes given that are important and not the individual nature of any of the packages in particular. It is appreciated that some packages may demonstrate the facilities and processes listed in more than one section.*	

237

Topic	Amplification	See Chapter
Database Management	Understand the concepts of files, records and fields including the terminology tables, rows and columns. Software used should allow: • the insertion and deletion of fields; • the insertion and deletion of records; • tables to be linked together; • the editing of information with records; • the validation of data on entry; • a simple search on one criterion only; • a complex search on two or more criteria; • the control of content of reports by selection of fields; • the control of the format of reports.	10
Spreadsheets	Software used should allow: • text, numbers and formulae to be entered into cells; • the insertion and deletion of columns and rows; • formatting of cells; • editing of entries within cells; • replication of cells; • the solution of 'what if' problems.	11
Charts	Software used should allow: • the construction of bar-charts, pie-charts and scatter graphs from tables of data; • labels on axes, legends and headings; • numbers scales on the axes to be edited;	11
Word processing	Software used should allow: • the movement, copying and deletion of blocks of text; • the alteration of margins and spacing; • the use of tabulation; • left, right, centred and full justification.	12
Mail-merging	Software used should allow the automatic production of documents, where each document contains standard text together with personalised information inserted at the same point within each document.	12

Topic	Amplification	See Chapter
Desk Top Publishing	Software used should allow: • text and graphics to be imported; • text and graphics to be positioned on the page; • text to be formatted, including changes in font type, style, and size.	**13**
Drawing	Software used should allow: • freehand drawing; • use of pre-defined shapes; • use of colour; • addition of text; • colour fills; • textured effects; • rotation of shapes.	**14**
Graphics	Software used should allow: • the use of brushes; • sections of the picture to be moved or copied, reflected and scaled; • images to be imported; • addition of text.	**14**
Web design	Software used should allow: • text and pictures to be imported; • the use of table to position text and graphics; • hyperlinks to be created from text and graphics; • hot spots to be placed over parts of pictures.	**20**
Modelling	Software used should allow an investigation involving changing variables. Examples of packages are: • a spreadsheet for financial modelling; • a city planning and development program; • a simple flight simulator.	**15**
9.7 Development of applications software	Understand that application software: • is written in a computer language; • can be configured to suit the particular preferences of users; • can be customised by altering the coding; • can be written to meet the specific needs of a user.	**9**

	Topic	Amplification	See Chapter
9.8	**Networks and communications**	Understand the difference between local area networks (LANs) and wide area networks (WANs). Discuss the advantages and disadvantages of use of networks as compared to stand-alone systems. Show awareness that a modem is required where telephone lines are used in communications systems. (Details of modulation are not required). Know about the advantages and disadvantages of ISDN compared to the use of modems. E-mail. Know about electronic mail, the facilities it has to offer, its use, advantages and disadvantages compared to fax, telephone and post.	**17, 18**
9.9	**Evaluation of major hardware and software components of systems**	Explain why particular hardware and software is appropriate for a particular task. Develop criteria for evaluating hardware and software.	
9.10	**Gathering data**		3
	When, where and why different methods of data capture are used	Understand the use of questionnaires, data capture forms, data logging, feedback, OMR, OCR, MICR, bar codes, and magnetic strips in gathering data.	
	Data logging	Know there is a range of sensors, which can be used to collect data. Show awareness that sensors can be calibrated to a known scale before use. Understand that data can be collected over long or short periods and that the logging interval can also be long or short. Know that data can be collected over short distances or over long distances. Understand that the data collected is stored and can be processed at a later stage.	
	Data validation	Know the reason for data validation. Know the following validation checks; range check, presence check, check digit, data type check, parity check and the type of errors each will detect and where they will be used.	4

	Topic	Amplification	See Chapter
9.11	**Storing data**		
	Data structures	Understand the concept of a database as a collection of stored data organised into files or data tables. Understand the nature and purpose of key fields. Understand how linking data tables can reduce the duplication of data making it easier to keep up to date and increasing the consistency of the data. Understand that data can be extracted from a database to produce many different reports and that data from different files in a database can be used to produce a single report.	**10**
	The implications of file size for data storage	Know that fields can be of different types and of fixed or variable lengths. Know the advantages and disadvantages of using fixed and variable length fields. Understand that files can be very large and that large files require a large backing store. Know that file compression can be used to reduce the size of some files but that these files have to be expanded before use. Know how encoding data in a suitable format affects file size and ease of data retrieval.	**10**
9.12	**Security of data**	Understand the physical precautions needed to protect media including protection from heat, magnetic fields, and water. Understand the need to restrict physical access to terminals and buildings. Describe the file generation back-up system and the use of file dumps and transaction log files for backup of on-line systems. Understand the use of passwords to prevent unauthorised access to data Show awareness of the use of encryption to prevent use of stolen data.	**21**
9.13	**Processing data**		
	Searching and matching	Understand the nature of the logical operators AND, OR and NOT as used in construction of database queries and filters.	**10**
	Sorting files	Know that the order of records depends in which order fields are chosen for sorting. Understand the importance of sorting a transaction file before merging with a master file.	

Topic	Amplification	See Chapter
Merging files	Understand that merging can be simple such as appending one file onto another provided that both contain the same set of fields. Understand that updating a master file requires a new file to be created from the merging of a transaction file with a current master file.	10
The different methods of processing data	Describe batch, real time, interactive and transaction processing and understand when the use of each is appropriate.	
Control	Understand that data acquired from sensors can be used to control devices and appreciate the importance of feedback in such systems.	23
9.14 **Presenting information**	Know that information can be presented on screen, as hard copy and in multimedia presentations and understand the need to select an appropriate presentation for a given application and audience. Understand that such presentations can include sound, text, pictures, graphs and charts.	
9.15 **Modelling and simulation**	Understand that a computer model is based on rules and that accuracy of the results produced is dependent on the extent to which the rules are true. Show awareness of the use of spreadsheets for financial modelling. Understand that realistic simulators such as flight simulators and virtual reality software also rely on rules built into the controlling software. Candidates will be expected to have had practical experience of the use of modelling software.	15
9.16 **The system life cycle**	Describe the steps involved in analysis, design, implementation and testing of a system. Understand the nature and purpose of feasibility studies, and the use of interviews, questionnaires and observation in analysis of existing or new systems. Understand the principles of top-down design of systems and be able to identify the subsystems required. Understand the purpose and nature of evaluation criteria. Show awareness that there may be more than one way of implementing a particular system and be able to discuss the advantages and disadvantages of alternative methods.	16

Topic		Amplification	See Chapter
		Understand the nature and purpose of a testing plan and be aware that testing must include typical, extreme and erroneous data. Describe the nature and purpose of documentation, which should be provided with a system.	16
9.17	Communications	Understand that data can be transmitted rapidly on a global basis. Understand the existence of global networks such as the Internet and the opportunities and problems presented by the use of such networks. Understand the use of web pages and search engines. Know the effects and implications of: • E-commerce, including the secure transfer of data • The use of on-line booking services • Global information and communication technology services. The following example is given to clarify what is meant by a global information and communication technology service: secretarial service; any other ICT service that can be undertaken with the supplier and customer in different countries is also covered. • The integration of digital television, web browsers, mobile telephones, digital cameras.	18
9.18	The Data Protection Act	Know the provisions of the 1998 Data Protection Act. Know that there is a requirement to register. Know the responsibilities of data users. Know the rights of data subjects. Know what are the full and partial exemptions to the act and their effects.	22
9.19	Data misuse	Understand why electronically-stored personal information is potentially easier to misuse than that kept in conventional form. Understand the effects of inaccurate data in files of personal information.	21

	Topic	Amplification	See Chapter
9.20	**Copyright law and anti-hacking legislation**	Show awareness that software cannot be copied without permission. Know of the consequences of software piracy. Show awareness of computer hacking and understand that it can lead to accidental or deliberate corruption of data.	**21**
9.21	**Growth of information and its effects on society**	Describe the use of information technology, and compare it with other methods. Understand that personal information may be held on computer, which is of interest to individuals and their families. Understand the impact of information technology on the lives of members of the community. Discuss the environmental, ethical, moral and social issues raised by information technology.	**22, 25**
9.22	**Health and safety**	Know that using a computer for a long time can affect people's health. Know what steps can be taken to help alleviate stress, eye strain, or wrist, back and neck problems, when using a computer for long periods. Know that there are regulations covering the use of computers in business and commerce to prevent injury to the users.	**24**

Index